"Unmuzzled provides a way of escape from the greatest threat to the cause of Christ today! Jeremy pulls no punches in this powerful and practical book on how to walk in freedom from sexual sin. Tragically, most Christian men are struggling. Unmuzzled exposes the danger of pornography, hidden sexual sin, and provides the Biblical roadmap like never seen before. Every man should read this book!"

JOSH D. MCDOWELL
Best-Selling Author of "Evidence That Demands a Verdict"
International Speaker and Christian Apologist

UNMUZZLED

J S SHELTON

ESCAPING SEXUAL SIN | SATAN'S GRIP ON MEN

BULK ORDERS / SPEAKING REQUESTS

Please email: bite@unmuzzledmen.com

UNMUZZLED

Published by: J.S.Shelton

Copyright © 2023 by J.S. Shelton. All rights reserved.

ISBN 978-1-7332158-0-0 (paperback edition)

ISBN 978-1-7332158-1-7 (electronic edition)

DISCLAIMER: This book is not a self-help book tailored to fit your personal feelings and beliefs. Stop here if you're unable to digest biblical truth.

Unless otherwise stated, all Scripture quotations are taken from *The Holy Bible, New King James Version*®. Copyright © 1982 by Thomas Nelson. Used by permission. All rights reserved. This is the version I grew up on! So if this isn't you're preferred version, I get it. However, don't let this stop you from digesting the Biblical truth in this book.

Scripture quotations marked NLT are taken from the *New Living Translation*, copyright © 1996, 2004, 2007 by Tyndale House Foundation. Used by permission of Tyndale House Publishers, Inc., Carol Stream, IL 60188. All rights reserved.

Scripture quotations marked NIV are taken from the *Holy Bible, New International Version*®, NIV®. Copyright © 1973, 1978, 1984, 2011 by Biblica, Inc.™ Used by permission of Zondervan. All rights reserved worldwide. www.zondervan.com. The "NIV" and "New International Version" are trademarks registered in the United States Patent and Trademark Office by Biblica, Inc.™

Any italic, bold, or underlined words in Scripture quotations are the author's additions for emphasis or clarity.

This is a non-fiction book and all stories are true. However, some names and identifying details have been changed to protect the privacy of individuals.

All references are categorized by chapter in the back of the book.

Cover design and typesetting by Scott Cornelius, www.scottcornelius.com

First printing 2019 / Revised 2023 /Printed in the United States of America.

Library of Congress Control Number: 2019909505

CONTENTS

PART 4   THE WARNING

PART 5   UNMUZZLED MEN

CONCLUSION

APPENDIX

DEDICATED TO

GOD
For my life and the redemption of it through Jesus Christ.

•

MY WIFE
For allowing me to become the spiritual leader of my home.

•

MY CHILDREN
May the Lord continue to help me train you up.

•

MY MOM & DAD
For doing whatever it took to raise and provide for me.

SPECIAL THANKS TO

MY FRIEND GARTH MERRICK
For loving, reproving, and encouraging me.

•

THE COOPER FAMILY
For the frequent use of their cabin to write this book.

•

JACK GIGL
For consistently encouraging me to deliver this message.

•

MY WIFE & KIDS
For the sacrifices you made for me to write this.

PART 1
SATAN'S NUMBER ONE ATTACK

CHAPTER 1
THE NSX

Just about any man who got a glimpse into his life was envious. I first met him when he came to utilize my vehicle brokerage service, a business I started in 2007 purely out of obedience to what I felt the Holy Spirit and the Word of God leading me to. Today, I know now it had nothing to do with cars and everything to do with the people He would send me–especially this young man.

Life was good. He had a loving wife, a promising career, and a new baby on the way. After helping him and his wife upgrade their vehicles, our paths crossed again several years later when he needed to sell a vehicle. Not just any vehicle, an Acura NSX.

Man, I'll admit it. I was envious of this guy. You see, the NSX had been a dream car of mine since I was a kid. In fact, weeks before meeting my wife in college, I had been working on a deal to purchase one from a guy in Florida. After saving for several years, I was finally able to zero in on one when this beautiful girl entered my life. She was the girl who caused me to get on my knees and ask, *God, is she the one?* As I was seeking the Lord, I was also trying to put this car deal together. Back then, buying a car sight-unseen from a private seller in another state, who posted a vehicle on some website called *eBay*, was a much riskier and more time-consuming venture than it is today. To help timestamp my point, I waited nearly three weeks for the seller to snail-mail me photographs! Digital cameras were just entering the world. Because of this, I couldn't just hit a *Buy Now* button, send over the money, and have it shipped to me. All this to say, I asked that girl to marry me before sealing the deal on the car.

Suddenly, something shifted inside me and a dream-crushing thought immediately crossed my mind. *Would it in any way be selfish of me to have this incredible, high-end car and keep my bride-to-be in her dilapidated Dodge Neon?* As much as I wanted to believe it wasn't my problem and her grandparents could easily supply her with another car, I couldn't shake it. Suddenly, all the money I saved over the years mowing yards and waiting tables, was not just mine anymore. I wasn't even married yet and was already feeling this *dying-to-self* my childhood pastor, Jimmy Evans, always spoke about in his marriage sermons. Needless to say, I never bought that NSX.

As he sat in my office to drop off his NSX, he said, "Once we sell this, I want you to help me locate my true dream car, a Lamborghini." I loved and envied this guy all in the same millisecond. He was a Christian, successful, had a wonderful family, and he had my car! As we wrapped up the details for selling it, I remember him emphasizing how pristine the car was. "This car has never seen a drop of rain." he said.

The next day, I couldn't wait to get to the office. On the agenda? A test drive and photo shoot with my dream car. After pulling it out of the warehouse, I still remember the puzzled reaction I had to the music coming from a CD he had left in it. I couldn't tell you who it was, but it was heavy secular music with explicit language. For a moment, I let the upgraded sound system pound and the feeling of "I am the man" infiltrate me as I shifted through the gears. Guys, you know the feeling. My ego was heightened, and I felt like a rock star. It's so easy to be overtaken by things like that. After laughing at myself, my next thought was: *Why is this Christian guy listening to such garbage*? Today, I look back at that moment with devastation in my soul. Why? I realize it was an opportunity God may have given me to grab hold of a man who was heading toward a slaughter (Proverbs 24:11). Back then, it didn't cross my mind God could be positioning me to intervene in this man's life.

Weeks later, a guy from Oregon called and a deal was struck on the NSX. With a sealed deal on the table, there was just one last step: Drive it home before it shipped out. This, of course, is part of my due diligence process to make sure all is well with a car before it ships out to the new owner. Not to mention, I wanted to drive it! There I was, finally driving my dream car, even if for just a day. As I walked out my front door the next morning, my client's words immediately flashed across my mind: *It's never seen a drop of rain.* Yep, it was pouring rain. I quickly convinced myself a little rainwater never hurt anything. In fact, within seconds, I had fully justified this NSX needed to experience some rain! Giddy up.

Driving an NSX in the pouring rain has nothing to do with the purpose of this story, but it did help permanently etch it into my mind. As I watched the transport truck carry it away, I remember standing there on the curb and whispering: "*Thank You, God.*" Not only was it a fantastic vehicle to have in my possession, but it was a profitable sale for both my client and me. At the time, it never crossed my mind I may have missed God's entire purpose behind it all. I would've never guessed the day I handed him the proceeds check would also be the last day I would see him. He assured me he'd be back soon to discuss sourcing his next dream car.

About a year later, I received a phone call from his wife. "Can you help us sell the Lexus we purchased from you awhile back?" she asked. "Of course, when would you like to drop it off?" I responded. "Could you instead pick it up from our house? It would really help me out," she inquired. This wasn't something I normally did, but I was willing to for this family. She gave me the address and then quickly hung up. Something wasn't right. First, why was his wife calling? Her husband always dealt with me before. Second, why was she so abrupt? As I struggled to discern her phone call, it literally crossed my mind to *Google* his name. What came up devastated me instantly: *Husband and father of three sentenced to sixty years in prison for possession and distribution of child pornography.*

A DIF-FERENT KIND OF SIN

CHAPTER 2

The flesh is not totally annihilated at conversion...the war goes on.

~ R.C. Sproul

In 2016 widely known evangelist, Josh McDowell, told CBN News, "I would personally say that from all my knowledge now, pornography is probably the greatest threat to the cause of Christ in the history of the world."

Pornography, the greatest threat to the cause of Christ? Wow, that's a severely strong statement, wouldn't you say? If true, shouldn't we be hearing about this? Shouldn't there be an alarm sounding off at every church in the world? Yes, yes, and yes! Are you ready for this? The reason we're not hearing any real noise is because most Christian men are in it! If anyone was going to sound the alarm, it would only be Christians.

CHRISTIAN MEN ARE AS ADDICTED TO PORNOGRAPHY AS NON-CHRISTIAN MEN.

Research conducted by Barna Research Group and Josh McDowell Ministries shows the number of Christian men who view pornography nearly mirrors that of non-Christian men. Think about this. Christian men are as addicted to pornography as non-Christian men. Today, we even have pastors falling left and right to what the church labels as "moral failures." Why are we trying to disguise it? The majority of them are "sexual failures."

Why isn't something drastic being done to sound the alarm? Don't get me wrong, I know there are pastors and leaders addressing this topic. There have been hundreds of books written and thousands of sermons preached on how to get free from pornography. Yet instead of witnessing an uprising, we are tolerating a backsliding. Why aren't we winning? As sons of a supernatural God, why have we become such a fruitless and passive representation of Him in this area? Sexual immorality inside the church is now just a few percentage points less than outside the church. Morality, in general, is declining. In a recent Lifeway Research poll, 81% of Americans said they were concerned with the declining moral behavior of our nation. If God calls and equips us to be set apart from this world and its lusts, why are most Christian men living sexually immoral lifestyles?

There are two primary factors contributing to this moral decline. First, the world is constantly advancing the availability, accessibility, and acceptance of sexual immorality.

According to a recent Gallup survey, 67% of men aged 18 to 49 now label pornography as morally acceptable. Even more disturbing, 50% of those who said religion was "fairly important" to them, also said porn was morally acceptable. Please catch this: The survey didn't ask if porn was acceptable, it asked whether it was "morally acceptable." If you're measuring your morality against today's societal acceptance, wake up. This is the same society who has proposed pedophilia may be a sexual orientation, not a crime.

Second, Christians frequently underscore God's Word and the role He plays in the battle between our flesh and spirit. Most of the time, we're not even considering His existence during sexual immorality. Most of the teachings, strategies, tactics, and books today focus on what *you* need to do to become free. In other words, what your mind, will, flesh, and circumstances need to become. Other than talking about how His grace covers you, I've found very little material speaking of God's role and provision for us in this battle.

Did you know sexual sin is different from all other sins? The Bible tells us *"Every sin that a man does is <u>outside</u> the body, but he who commits sexual immorality sins against his <u>own</u> body"* (1 Corinthians 6:18). Right there in the Bible we are plainly told sexual sin is unique. This sin spiritually and physically incapacitates us. Satan has been using sex against man since the beginning of time. 2 Corinthians 10:4 says, *"The weapons of our warfare are not carnal."* Ephesians 6:12 tells us, *"We do not wrestle against flesh and blood, but against principalities, against powers, against the rulers of the darkness of this age, against spiritual hosts of wickedness in the heavenly places."* So, as flesh and spirit beings, if our spirit is overcome by our flesh, we lose. Make no mistake about it. Satan has identified sexual sin as his number one weapon and he is constantly using it to incapacitate us.

I think most Christians hide sexual immorality because they hoped or believed once saved, their carnal desire would disappear. Or when they got married, they would only desire sex with their wife. When they realize their fleshly desires, tendencies, and thoughts still exist, many put on a religious act by sweeping their sins under the rug. Hiding sin entirely misuses grace! Christians who end up here become expert preachers on God's unending grace. Substituting grace for obedience has become a common practice in the church today. It's how a pastor or church leader can sin sexually and then go preach and pray for people all in the same day. Sadly, men who end up here are in a constant holding pattern. The only way these men can "land their plane" is if they overcome sexual sin.

SUBSTITUTING GRACE FOR OBEDIENCE HAS BECOME A COMMON PRACTICE IN THE CHURCH TODAY.

Today, we are entering a time in history when, if you don't get free now, you may never get free. In this book, I will reveal a time-sensitive warning to all believers.

Christians are Satan's target and his weapon of choice is sex. Here are three reasons why:

1. He knows you were created as a sexual being. (Genesis 2:24)
2. He knows sexual immorality incapacitates us. (1 Corinthians 6:18)
3. He knows shame causes us to hide from God. (Genesis 3:10)

Picture yourself signing up for the front-line infantry when you decide to follow Christ. Now, I'm not talking about someone who claims to be a Christian and goes to church on Easter and Christmas only. News flash: This type of Christian is not a threat to Satan. I'm talking about men who march down the path of becoming all God has created them to be and men who sell out to God's plan for their life. These men are Satan's targets. As followers of Christ, God has amazing plans for each of us. If Satan can strike you with sexual sin, he can stifle God's plan for you.

SEXUAL IMMORALITY IS ANY SEXUAL AROUSAL OUTSIDE A COVENANT MARRIAGE.

Allow me to state a personal definition: *Sexual immorality is any sexual arousal outside a covenant marriage.* Any action or thought. Today, the main source for sexual temptation and immorality is the Internet. Whether it's pornography, sexual content, solicitation for sex, or social media, the Internet is the primary portal where most men sin sexually. Outside the Internet, this means anything or anyone that activates a sexual arousal in you. Men, we must be on guard every time we step foot into the world. Today, you don't have to seek out sexual temptation, it will seek you out. When the Bible instructs us to put on the *"full armor of God"* in Ephesians 6, it isn't simply so we can look like Christians. It's because we're not of this world and we desperately need it!

We are in a sexual war, and the enemy is winning this battle in the souls of millions of men. The truths contained in this book assume you are a follower of Jesus Christ. If you're not, I commend you for seeking freedom from sexual immorality and I encourage you to read on. I believe God will reveal Himself to you. The message contained in this book is unlike any other "get free from porn" message out there. How so? It relies exclusively on God's Word and His supernatural power.

You will never win this battle by your own will, grit, or determination. Attempting to wrestle or deal with sexual temptation is the same as walking into a blazing inferno expecting your flesh to suddenly become fireproof. The Bible clearly tells us this battle will require obedience to God's directives and reliance on His supernatural intervention.

For the weapons of our warfare are not carnal but mighty in God for pulling down strongholds, casting down arguments and every high thing that exalts itself against the knowledge of God, bringing every thought into captivity to the obedience of Christ, and being ready to punish all disobedience when your obedience is fulfilled.
(2 Corinthians 10:4-6)

Did you know your flesh wasn't designed to withstand sexual temptation? The Bible tells us we cannot take fire and expect it not to burn us (Proverbs 6:27-28). The "fire" in this verse is referring to a sexual temptation. Yet, finding a way to physically withstand or resist fire is the very foundation of the teachings and biblical interpretations given to those who struggle with sexual sin today. Retraining your eyes, software protection, accountability, or that you can be supernaturally healed from temptation–these techniques only deceive a man into thinking he can become fireproof. It's why most of the "get free from porn" techniques eventually fizzle out. It's how men become free one day and fall miserably the next. It's why every single pastor in the world who should be leading this battle, isn't. You can't give what you don't have! If you never actually conquer, how can you teach others to conquer? This book will plainly lay out the biblical directives that yield freedom from sexual immorality. Otherwise, I'd be wasting your time and mine.

Sexual sin is restraining men all over the world, especially in the church. Here is the visual metaphor of this book: A Christian man in sexual sin, is muzzled. This muzzle renders him passive and powerless to participate in the Kingdom of God on this earth. It prevents him from becoming the man, husband, father, and witness he is called to be. This spiritual restraint mutes his connection to God. Worse, it incapacitates a man from fulfilling his God-given purpose. God is constantly reaching out to him, but sexual sin consistently binds him from reaching out to God.

I encourage you to read this book from start to finish. Don't jump around or skim through it. The next ten chapters set the stage and prepare you to receive biblical truth. It is written to a man who genuinely desires to go all-in with God. With that said, it won't comfort or excuse you, but rather challenge and equip you.

SEXUAL SIN IS RESTRAINING MEN ALL OVER THE WORLD, ESPECIALLY IN THE CHURCH.

CHAPTER 3
THE MUZZLE

When you want to help people,
you tell them the truth.

- Thomas Sowell

In his study, *The Effects of Pornography on Marriage*, Dr. Patrick Fagan puts it this way: "Pornography undermines everything we try to achieve as husbands and fathers." Let that soak in for a bit. It's the primary reason men aren't succeeding in the headship role to which God has called them (1 Corinthians 11:3). How can you speak God's Word, declare His promises, or truly seek and cry out to God if your mouth is tied shut? Imagine a muzzle wrapped around your jaw and face so tightly you couldn't even open your lips enough to speak. Leonard Ravenhill nailed it when he said, "No man is greater than his prayer life." Meaning, you will never become the man you are called and created to be without constantly and consistently communicating with God.

I shared the imagery of a muzzle with a friend of mine who served in the United States Navy. As he pictured this attack from the enemy, he immediately likened a Christian man to the military term: HVT, or *High Value Target*. For example, during the Iraq War, Osama Bin Laden was an HVT to the United States Military. Christian men who commit to become all God has called them to be instantly become HVTs to Satan. His goal? Take them out.

Why use the imagery of a muzzle to illustrate a man in sexual sin? Because it's what I see as I've encountered countless Christian men who've made me scratch my head and ask: *Why aren't you pressing into God? Why is your wife the one leading? Why are you not praying with your wife? Why are you not acting as the spiritual leader of your home? Why are you not in spiritual warfare for your children? Why are you not on your knees asking God for help in times of need? Why are you standing in the middle of a church worship service like a dead man? Why are you so passive and timid if you claim to be a son of God?*

Just as a muzzle incapacitates a dog, sexual sin incapacitates a man. A muzzled man feels restricted and unworthy to pray, seek, and speak to God. Sure, he may rise up on some days and declare he is no longer going to wear it, surrender to God, and receive grace and forgiveness. Most men become experts in this habitual process. But, until a man takes a permanent stance and allows grace to *transform* him versus *excuse* him, freedom is cyclical at best. The enemy always aims to re-muzzle a man as quickly as possible. I meet these guys often and ask, "Hey, do you struggle with pornography?" My question is right to the point and requires an immediate response. Unfortunately, the answer is yes almost every time. If the answer is no, it's usually, "I used to, but I got free from it." "Really, tell me when and how?" I inquire. "Well, I recently got set free and committed my purity to the Lord." Or, "God finally healed me." Or, "I have an accountability partner now."

"When did this happen?" I ask. The usual response is, "It's been about a month now." A few years ago, I asked a guy when he last looked at pornography. He proudly said, "It's been nearly three full months now." Meeting him for breakfast a few months later, I learned he had once again fallen back into it.

GOD ISN'T SATISFIED FOR YOU TO CONTINUOUSLY BE ON A "SIN-REPENT-SIN" CYCLE.

Men, God isn't satisfied for you to continuously be on a "sin-repent-sin" cycle while on this earth. Get off that mouse wheel. We serve a God who calls us to conquer. He put us here and gave us life through Jesus Christ to be masters of this world, not slaves. Revelation 3:21 states, *"To him who overcomes I will grant to sit with Me on My throne, as I also overcame and sat down with My Father on His throne."* Have you ever considered that He expects us to overcome sin?

If so, you must believe He provided a way to do it, right? Many Christian men I meet believe they will struggle in this area the rest of their lives, as if it's just part of being a man. Many of these same men believe they can live with some degree of sexual sin and still become all God called them to be. Let me say this in love: WRONG. These men are like dogs chained to a stake. They will never reach their destiny on this earth.

These are often men who genuinely desire to reach their full potential as the men God created them to be, yet year after year, they find themselves stuck in the same spot they've always been. Their muzzles keep them from God's true blessings. There are a growing number of pastors who are no different. They are ignorantly unaware sin has cut the power out of their ministry. They may have a large following, but they are quietly leading their flock right off a lukewarm cliff. Don't misinterpret what I'm saying here, I have confidence all believers desire to be in right standing with God. However, their sin prevents them from doing so. Isaiah 59:2 says, *"But your iniquities have separated you from your God; and your sins have hidden His face from you, so that He will not hear."* Men, it's time to wake up. Sexual sin will restrict you from reaching the fullness of God's plan for your life. Think about this: The Israelites wondered in the desert for forty years on a journey that should have taken them about eleven days. Why? Disobedience.

Let me stop here and say a few things before you continue. First, this book may punch you in the gut or cut deep into your soul. Why? Because it's a message to alert men they could be on a road heading toward a slaughter (Proverbs 24:11). I challenge you to suppress your flesh and allow your spirit to digest the biblical truth within, even if it hurts. This is a strategic war directive for true believers who are ready to own up to sexual immorality and destroy it. It wasn't written to kick you down–it was written to pull you up.

Second, this book is written to men. This is not to say women cannot read or benefit from it. Today, women are struggling with sexual sin at an alarming rate. If you're a woman and feel drawn to this book, please read and apply it in your life. It contains biblical truth for all of God's children. But consider this thought. If the men of this world were walking in accordance and obedience to the Word of God, would women have ever become entangled in this trap to begin with? Women who struggle sexually have typically been abused, manipulated, or neglected by a man. Unrighteous men are the common denominator amongst women in sexual bondage today.

WET MATCHES

CHAPTER 4

*This is no time for wimpy Christians.
It's time for soldiers of Christ to arise!*

~Alistair Begg

When I was young boy, I would often be up in my treehouse playing with matches. Something about striking a match gave me a thrill and made me feel older than I was. So, every time we visited a restaurant or place that gave away those paper matchbooks, I'd sneak a handful of them when no one was looking. Then, I'd stash them in an old coffee can I hid in my treehouse. One day, after a good ol' west Texas rain, I headed into the backyard to play. Climbing up the ladder, I noticed my coffee can had fallen over and all my matchbooks were in a puddle of water.

Have you ever tried to light a wet match? Its outward appearance can fool you. It looks like a match and still has everything needed to fulfill its purpose as a match. However, if it's wet, it won't light. Furthermore, if it stays wet too long, it may never fire and fulfill its purpose. Due to what it's soaked in, it's a powerless dud.

Picture a man who does whatever his flesh desires, douses his sin with a so-called "grace" and then declares, "I'm a Christian." These men have hidden sexual sin in their past and usually continue to habitually sin. However, they are fully convinced they're in good standing with God. Unlike a man who is remorseful of his sin, and genuinely desires to be freed from it, these men are *wet matches*. They look like Christians, act like Christians, and can even sing and dance to fool you in to believing they're Christians. But due to what they're soaked in, they cannot catch fire for the Lord. Today, the church is *flooded* with them.

Even so you also outwardly appear righteous to men, but inside you are full of hypocrisy and lawlessness.
Matthew 23:28

Is it possible a man who claims to be a Christian, reads the Bible, attends church, is in ministry, or is even a pastor can so easily fall to sexual sin? First, I've yet to meet a man with "fireproof flesh." Second, not only is it possible, it's becoming more likely. We live in a world of rapidly increasing sexual immorality with an adversary who is hell-bent on destroying Christians. As Proverbs 7:26-27 states, the attack is on *"strong men."* Wake up, believers. As Christians, we're not immune to sexual temptation–we're the enemy's number one target for it.

Most Christians who struggle with sexual immorality live as if God has said, *"Men, I designed you to be sexually attracted to women. However, I only allow you to be sexual with one woman– your wife. So, good luck staying pure!"* Listen up. Luck has nothing to do with it. What God creates, He sustains. So, would God create a sexual being, call it sexually weak, demand obedience against sexual immorality, yet not offer a way to achieve it? A large percentage of Christian men end up believing this. Why? Because they continue to struggle. Many have exhausted every tactic and strategy only to fall again. Please catch this. This is the primary reason why men hide and deny they struggle sexually at all. In other words, they move from mourning sin to coping with sin. It's how a man can spend the night in porn, go to church the next morning, and high-five God for washing him clean. However, until he conquers sin, versus continually drowning in what Bonhoeffer called "cheap grace," or "grace without Jesus Christ," he will remain a dud.

1 Corinthians 6:9-10 tells us, *"Neither idolaters or adulterers will inherit the Kingdom of God."* Men who declare that God accepts their ongoing sin qualify as both. Adulterers because of their sexual sin, idolaters because they worship a false god. The God of the Bible is against all sin. A man who has justified ongoing sin by declaring God's leniency through the misuse and misappropriation of grace, is worshiping a false god. To believe that God, the one who commands fathers to train and discipline their children, is a Father who would enable His children with some unlimited grace-card, is foolishness and unbiblical.

Not everyone who says to Me, "Lord, Lord," shall enter the kingdom of heaven, but he who does the will of My Father in heaven. Many will say to Me in that day, "Lord, Lord, have we not prophesied in Your name, cast out demons in Your name, and done many wonders in Your

name?" And then I will declare to them, "I never knew you; depart from Me, you who practice lawlessness!"
Matthew 7:21-23

A serious epidemic is infiltrating the church today. It's become normal to hear, "Yeah, I'm a Christian" right out of the mouth of a person who speaks profanity, has an affair, watches filth and is regularly immersed in the lusts of this world. Even worse, we are seeing a new wave of Christians who believe they can "white-out" what they don't agree with in the Bible. These so-called Christians have become so comfortable misusing God's grace, they raise their hands in worship and somehow sing and shout praises to the Lord–all while habitually sinning. This is thwarting true revival in the body of Christ today. I highly recommend *Why Revival Tarries* by Leonard Ravenhill if you want to dive deeper into the spiritual condition of the church today.

Years ago, I felt the Holy Spirit lead me to talk to a certain man at church one morning. I admit, my flesh didn't want to. However, I couldn't deny the discernment I had toward him. His confession? He had just committed adultery. Looking back, I know God used that moment to awaken him from his foolishness. Although this guy was at church worshipping, God's hands were tied from doing anything in his life.

A man who is drowning cannot say he is saved from the water while he is sinking in it.
- Charles Spurgeon

In Genesis, when God established a new covenant with Noah, He promised never to flood the earth again to destroy all flesh. In Matthew 5:45, we learn *"He makes His sun rise on the evil and on the good, and sends rain on the just and on the unjust."* Combine these two passages, and you might conclude that you can go on living comfortably, go to church or not go to church, believe in God or not believe in God, and still have a decent life on this earth. Please catch this: Just because God hasn't struck you dead over your continued disobedience or sin, doesn't mean anything! Many Christian men think because their life is going well, their sexual sin must not be as big of a deal as the Bible states. They declare and proudly accept "the good" in their lives as God's blessings. This is a huge win for Satan. So many Christians in this world believe because they have good things happening in their lives, His grace must allow Him to overlook their continued sin. This is exactly where the enemy wants to keep you: In a life with enough "good" on the surface that prevents you from going all in with God's Word. We mistake "good" for "God." The truth is, when you're in sin, you can tie God's hands from truly blessing you. Worse, you unwittingly give Satan access to plunder your life. Never disregard the scriptures: *"The thief does not come except to steal, and to kill, and to destroy. I have come that they may have life, and that they may have it more abundantly"* (John 10:10).

One of the subcontractors I frequently use in my business told me years ago he had an affair and never intends to tell his wife. He was extremely regretful but said he knew, through God's grace, he was forgiven. Knowing this man, I believed he had genuinely repented and God did forgive him. Regardless, I still encouraged him to confess to his wife. Sadly, to my knowledge, he has yet to do so. Today, when I ask him about life, he declares God is good and he is blessed. To every husband who has undisclosed sin, past or present, do you honestly believe God simply overlooks the deception you cast over His daughter (your wife) every day? I'm not talking about forgiveness. I'm talking about expecting God to coexist with darkness. If you trap darkness in your marriage, you close it off from God to bless it. An unconfessed affair, a struggle with pornography- or any unconfessed sexual sin, traps darkness in your marriage. Scripture tells us, *"For everyone practicing evil hates the light and does not come to the light, lest his deeds should be exposed"* (John 3:20).

If this is you, I'm not writing to condemn you, but rather to alert you. Eradicate all darkness from your life while you still have the chance. Although the message of this book is specific to sexual sin, I encourage you to eradicate **all** unconfessed sin. A friend of mine who read this book prior to its release told me this section greatly convicted him. He didn't have any hidden sexual sin, but for years he had been lying to his wife about their finances. He immediately confessed and has since shared several testimonies with me about what God is doing in their marriage and their finances.

Righteousness is the primary marker of the Fathers DNA in you.
~ Tom Pennington

If you remain in sin or hold onto unconfessed sin, you will halt God's full destiny for your life. According to Proverbs 28:13, *"He who covers his sins will not prosper, but whoever confesses and forsakes them will have mercy."* Until you fully confess all your sins and stop misappropriating grace, you will drift further away from the plan God has for you. God's grace is freely available to all who repent. We serve the creator of mercy and grace and His supply is endless. I wonder if too many Christian men simply misunderstand grace. These men continually fulfill their sinful desires, declare themselves Christians, and then apply grace to wipe themselves clean. God's grace isn't hand sanitizer—it's the blood of Christ!

Allow me to reinforce this truth once more—specifically to men who have hidden or unconfessed sin in their marriage. You are ignorant to think God is smiling down on you if His daughter (your wife) is imprisoned in your darkness. If you are hiding sin from your spouse, you are keeping God out of your marriage. God's light will not coexist with darkness. God's grace is a doorway that allows His light to access the dark areas of your life. Surrendering all to Him is what obliterates the darkness. Confessing all sins to your spouse confirms you've surrendered to Him. James 4:6 reminds us, *"God resists the proud, but gives grace to the humble."* If you're not willing to humbly confess all your sins to

CONFESSING ALL SINS TO YOUR SPOUSE CONFIRMS YOU'VE SURRENDERED TO HIM.

your spouse, you're choosing to keep Him out of your marriage. Without His presence in your life, you'll remain a powerless dud to the Kingdom of God while on this earth.

The Lord is far from the wicked, but He hears the prayer of the righteous.
Proverbs 15:29

A man who is no longer remorseful over his sinful behavior is a *wet match*. He uses God's grace like a quick hand sanitizer after knowingly and willfully sinning. He approaches God something like this: *"What's up G-man! I sinned again. Grace, grace.* *Fist-bumps God* *Amen."* The Word clearly tells us we should mourn sin. *"Come near to God and he will come near to you. Wash your hands, you sinners, and purify your hearts, you double-minded.*

Grieve, mourn and wail. Change your laughter to mourning and your joy to gloom" (James 4:8-9).

CHAPTER 5

GRACE INVITES GOD IN

Grace is that which brings me to love God; and if I love God, I long to keep His commandments.

- Martyn Lloyd-Jones

When I was nine years old, I outran a police officer patrolling my neighborhood early one Saturday morning. Maybe my parents were telling the truth when they said it was against the law for me to ride my go-kart on the street. I assumed they made it up to keep me contained in our backyard. I must've piled up a thousand miles back there. I even created some banked turns from all the dirt I spread around once I figured out how to drift. I felt like a Bobby Allison or Jeff Gordon pinned behind a pace car as I tore up the yard week after week. I craved more speed and some straightaways! Restlessly lying in bed one Friday night, I devised a plan.

Most weekends I was usually up hours before anyone else and spent most of those mornings watching cartoons and eating junk food. Convinced my plan would work, I decided to go for it. All I had to do was push my go-kart out the back gate and down the alleyway far enough to get it started without waking up my mom or dad. After a few laps around the neighborhood, I'd kill the engine at the top of the street and coast back down to our gate. Our street had enough of an incline to pull it off.

When I saw a police car turn around in the distance behind me, I quickly sensed that whole "illegal" thing my mom always fed me might be true! Thinking back, either God caused him to appear out of nowhere, or a neighbor called the police early that morning. Looking over my shoulder, I'm not sure if it was the thought of going to jail at nine years old, or the fear of my parents finding out that triggered my next decision. Either way, it was a decision that would have a lasting impact on me for many years. Instead of surrendering, I made a quick drifting turn around the corner to the next street. I immediately spotted a house with an open garage. Now I didn't know who lived there, but without hesitation, I pulled right in and closed the garage door. Thinking back, I'm sure glad the homeowner never came out. In the small Texas town I grew up in, I could've been shot on the spot! As I peeked through the garage window, I saw the patrol car slowly pass by with the officer looking all over for me. Wow, I did it. I got away with it.

By seven o'clock, I was safely back home watching Saturday morning cartoons. What I didn't realize was a deposit embedded itself inside me that morning. A deposit that would lead me to further bend the rules and disregard authorities in my life. Eventually, I believed I could even hide from and disobey God and His Word—all while going to church and professing to be a Christian. Like most Christian men I meet with and counsel today, I both hid and justified my sin.

Neither the police nor my parents ever found out about that incident or any of the other early morning joy rides that followed. Sadly, the more I did it, the more desensitized and confident I became. I would go on to hide in many areas of my life, especially sexual sin. Why do Christians believe they can "get away" with sin? Maybe like I did, they believe grace simply excuses them.

God's grace is the only sufficiency to cover our sins. His grace redeems us, it's enough, and it is never-ending. Ephesians 1:7 says, *"In Him we have redemption through His blood, the forgiveness of sins, according to the riches of His grace."* In the previous chapter, I referenced 1 Corinthians 6:9-10 (specifically, where it calls out idolaters and adulterers). Now look at verse 11: *"And such were some of you. But you were washed, but you were sanctified, but you were justified in the name of the Lord Jesus and by the Spirit of our God."* It's amazing how this verse demonstrates God's grace. In other words, if you *were* once an idolater or an adulterer, the power of His grace alone redeems you.

The argument in this book is not about the purpose, the power, the availability, or the sufficiency of grace. Instead, it's about the twisted misuse of it in today's Christian culture. If the hand sanitizer analogy in the previous chapter didn't drive it home, let me say it this way: God never intended His Son's blood to be some "morning after pill."

So God created man in His own image; in the image of God He created him; male and female He created them.
Genesis 1:27

"To him who overcomes I will grant to sit with Me on My throne, as I also overcame and sat down with My Father on His throne."
Revelation 3:21

Combine these two passages and you will see that we are created, equipped, and expected to conquer. The enemy's strategy to destroy men with sexual sin is working. In this fallen world, we have an enemy who has been given jurisdiction and sexual sin is his weapon of choice on men. This is exactly why God gave us instructions in His Word to overcome it. The purpose of His grace is to redeem, restore, and relaunch us to complete this life–not to enable us to "live it up" and excuse our shortcomings to the finish-line. In Romans six, Paul clearly tells us misusing grace to justify the continuation of sin is completely contrary to the Word of God.

What shall we say then? Shall we continue in sin that grace may abound? Certainly not! How shall we who died to sin live any longer in it?
Romans 6:1-2

A WORD REGARDING ACCOUNTABILITY

Muzzled men become skilled at hiding. This is why accountability yields so much freedom initially. It gives a man an outlet from his otherwise full-time hiding. It allows him the chance to lay down his muzzle and become completely free with another believer. Accountability is healthy and a fantastic step toward purity. However, it's too often confused as a primary solution for sexual purity.

Many men who maintain a long-term accountability partner continue to struggle with sexual sin. They mistakenly label confession-of-sin for freedom-from-sin. Their confession erases the remorse they once carried. Instead of conquering sin, these men often become *wet matches*. They look and act like Christians, but are powerless duds. Let me also include men here who have struggled in the past, but are currently walking in freedom after confessing and becoming accountable to their wives. Many of these men have told me: "The thought of having to re-confess to my wife has

MISUSING GRACE TO JUSTIFY THE CONTINUATION OF SIN IS COMPLETELY CONTRARY TO THE WORD OF GOD.

been enough to keep me clean." Let me voice a warning here. Spousal accountability is healthy and appropriate. However, it's not the solution. The solution is to move from a fear-of-confession *tactic*, to a love-of-the-Lord *lifestyle*. When a man truly goes all-in with God, he is no longer content to merely confess sin, he becomes vigilant toward conquering it.

Jesus didn't die on the cross so we could cope with sin. He died so we could conquer sin.

~ **Jimmy Evans**

Sexual sin is not the only thing preventing you from fulfilling God's purpose for your life, but it has proven to be enough. This is why I personally believe it's the enemy's number one attack against us. He has discovered the lure of sexual sin is his best shot, especially with men. It yields massive dividends in Hell and continues to wreak havoc in the fulfillment of God's plan and purpose for our lives. When evangelist Josh McDowell issued a statement declaring, "*pornography is the greatest threat to the cause of Christ in the history of the world,*" this is what he was talking about. The church today isn't willing to admit that the majority of the men sitting in the congregation are muzzled porn addicts. Yes, I said *the majority* and yes, I said *addicts.* Don't believe for another second God is satisfied with you riding some grace train to the finish line. His grace empowers us, not enables us.

Let the wicked forsake his way, and the unrighteous man his thoughts; Let him return to the Lord, and He will have mercy on him; And to our God, for He will abundantly pardon.
Isaiah 55:7

If you're a man who believes the lie that you will always struggle and never conquer sexual sin, you have been deceived by the master deceiver and the number one enemy of God: Satan. Renew your mind of who your Father is by reading His Word. Get ready for His grace to transform you and unmuzzle you from Satan's grip. If you're the man I've likened to a wet match, get ready to reignite for the Lord. Psalm 55:22 encourages, "*Cast your burden on the Lord, And He shall sustain you; He shall never permit the righteous to be moved.*" Men, you must learn to stand behind God to shield yourselves from the enemy's attack on you. In the latter part of this book, I talk about a coming catastrophe that will sexually slaughter millions of men. Caution: Don't jump ahead or you will likely miss the spark needed to ignite you against it.

God's grace is no substitute for obedience. Quit believing the lie that you're under God's grace simply because you call yourself a Christian. He never intended grace to enable you in a lifestyle of sin. If His grace isn't transforming you, you're misusing it. Grace invites God in, not excuses Him out.

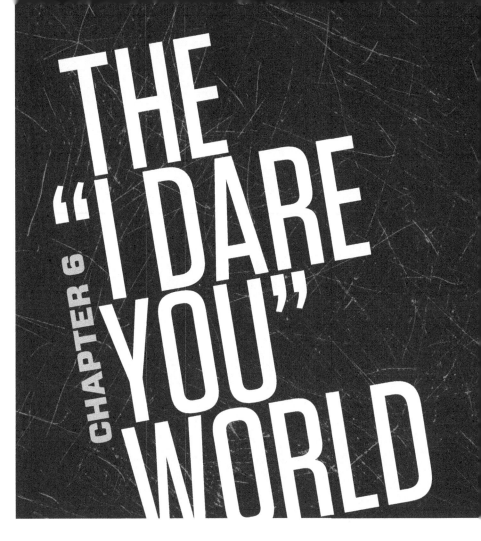

CHAPTER 6

THE "I DARE YOU" WORLD

In 2016, a high school kid was arrested and charged with a felony and sixty-nine misdemeanor counts of indecent exposure. Why? On a dare from his buddies, he exposed himself in a team football photo. While the moral standard of our world is in the gutter, the governing authorities felt fully justified to publicly humiliate and label this kid unfit for society. Not only was he charged, he was issued an ankle monitor to wear during the investigation. The world that promotes, encourages, and lures you into sexual immorality, is the same world waiting to destroy you once you're in it.

I'm not saying this young man's behavior was acceptable or should go unpunished. However, this clearly illustrates the "I dare you" nature of the world we live in today. If, in fact, showing your penis in a photograph is such a major crime in society, why haven't we seen something really done about it? Why haven't the same authorities that charged this young man not outlawed all the filth freely accessible in their jurisdiction? Why aren't they going after the pornography industry or public movie theaters that are literally showing pornography in films? What about video game stores that sell games full of sexual content to children? What about strip clubs that post massive sexual billboards along public highways for all to see? What about the internet that is full of sexual content? Is the world really against sexual immorality or does it only occasionally act like it is?

Recently, my son and I went to Bass Pro Shop for some man-time. At least once a month, he and I embark on a day of father and son adventures. Soon after entering the store, he spotted an arcade game near the indoor gun range. As we approached it, a promotional video was playing on the screen to entice people to play. The enticement? A provocatively dressed woman, sexually caressing her body. Really?! It was a hunting game! What kind of messed up society are we living in?

This world turns a blind eye to all the sexual filth and immorality we are inundated with every day, yet it's ready to pounce on and destroy all who engage or participate in it. The world tells us to come in, stay and play, soak it up, and have fun. What you don't see or hear is Satan's plan behind the scenes: *Once I get a foothold, get them hooked, desensitized, addicted, and coming back for more, they will soon cross the line. Then I will take them out. No mercy. Destroy them.*

You know those opening copyright/piracy warnings preceding the opening credits of every movie?

CHAPTER 6 | THE "I DARE YOU" WORLD

"Unauthorized use can lead to criminal charges including a felony, accompanied by up to five years in prison and fines up to $250,000. Reproduction and/or redistribution of this material is against Federal Law."

It's standard on most movies, right? Furthermore, most movies today are packed full of crime, drugs, sexual immorality, theft, conspiracy, murder, lust, and all sorts of criminal and immoral activity, right? Let me give you the real interpretation of this worldly warning: *Go ahead. Watch this movie we packed full of unlawful and immoral activity. Enjoy yourself doing it. However, if you dare to perform an unlawful act by copying it, we will take you down.* The world that promotes, encourages, and lures you with immorality in movies, video games, and the

THE EVIL YOU ALLOW TO FEED YOUR FLESH IS QUIETLY DEVOURING YOUR SOUL.

internet, is the same world waiting to destroy you with it. Then they will label you unfit for society. Do you not see the enemy is behind all of this? *Watch, play, and partake as often as you want. Have your fill of this garbage. Continue going deeper and deeper into it. Once you're desensitized, I'll take you down!* I can't tell you how many times I've witnessed a man fall to temptation while believing he could look and not touch. Know this: The evil you allow to feed your flesh is quietly devouring your soul. The more you engage in immoral activities, the less sensitivity you will have against them.

Beloved, I beg you as sojourners and pilgrims, abstain from fleshly lusts which <u>war</u> against the soul.
1 Peter 2:11

Abstain from every form of evil.
1 Thessalonians 5:22

In his interview with Dr. James Dobson the night before his execution, mass rapist and serial killer Ted Bundy said, "Society condemns Ted Bundy while they walk past a magazine rack full of the things that send kids down the road to one day becoming a Ted Bundy." Following the interview, society ridiculed, mocked, and chastised Mr. Bundy for blaming his horrific crimes on "harmless" magazines. At the end of 2017, society was given another illustration of this "harmless" claim. Read the following excerpt taken from Wikipedia in November 2017:

Harvey Weinstein is an American film producer and former film executive. He and his brother, Bob, co-founded Miramax. Their entertainment company produced several independent films including Sex, Lies, and Videotape (1989); The Crying Game (1992); Pulp Fiction (1994); Heavenly Creatures (1994); Flirting with Disaster (1996); and Shakespeare in Love (1998). Weinstein won an Academy Award for producing Shakespeare in Love, and garnered seven Tony Awards for a variety of plays and musicals, including The Producers, Billy Elliot the Musical, and August: Osage County. Weinstein was co-chairman of The Weinstein Company from 2005 to 2017. In October 2017, following numerous allegations of sexual harassment, sexual assault, and rape, Weinstein was fired by his company's board of directors and expelled from the Academy of Motion Picture Arts and Sciences.

When the news regarding the actions of Mr. Weinstein broke, the world instantly attacked him. Blind to the schemes of Satan and this world we live in, the same people who praised this man for his immoral films, now labeled him a sick and demented human being. The actors and actresses who willingly accepted roles in his movies full of sex, crime, and other worldly lusts were some of the first to condemn him. In the days following the news of Mr. Weinstein, a floodgate burst open with similar sexual allegations against hundreds of other celebrities and entertainment producers. Suddenly, the same society who applauded and eagerly devoured the entertainment garbage these men produced, began yelling for their heads!

Our society may appear to be lawfully against sexual immorality, but do not be deceived. Allow me to pull this curtain completely back to reveal how oblivious the world is today. Approximately two weeks before society scoffed at Mr. Weinstein and the many others exposed for sexual misconduct, this same society mourned the loss of, paid tribute to, and celebrated the life of the very man credited with normalizing pornography, Hugh Hefner. Wait, there's more. Just days following the death of Mr. Hefner, a massacre happened in Las Vegas, Nevada. A lone gunman killed more than fifty people and injured hundreds more. During the investigation, it was reported that the gunman had an intense addiction to pornography. Society's response? Gun control.

How about porn control?! Are we so deceived, blind, or simply unwilling as a society to look at what the Bible says about the destructive power of sexual sin? I'm pleading with you to detach yourself from this world and its lusts. We have an adversary whose only purpose is to steal, kill, and destroy (John 10:10). Wake up, men of God! It's time for believers to start believing in the existence of Satan as much as they believe in the existence of God! How disguised has the enemy become? Only those who choose to walk in full obedience to Biblical commands will recognize the disguised enemy of this world today. Everyone else will continue to be blind to his schemes.

Okay. Most of you reading this are likely thinking: *My sexual sin is nowhere near what I just read.* Sure, you may have never raped a woman, cheated on your spouse, or consumed child pornography, but please hear this loud and clear: This world isn't leading you to the gates of Heaven, it's pushing you to the gates of Hell. Do not be fooled. If you're engaged in any form of sexual immorality, you're playing with a fire designed to one day consume you. The Bible clearly warns:

THIS WORLD ISN'T LEADING YOU TO THE GATES OF HEAVEN, IT'S PUSHING YOU TO THE GATES OF HELL.

If you were of the world, the world would love its own. Yet because you are not of the world, but I chose you out of the world, therefore the world hates you.
John 15:19

No one engaged in warfare entangles himself with the affairs of this life, that he may please him who enlisted him as a soldier.
2 Timothy 2:4

Do you believe these scriptures enough to live by them? If so, what are you doing to walk in alignment with them? Are you entangled in something of this world? What part of the world and its values are you allowing into your life, your spouse's life, or your children's life? Speaking of parenting, who are you trusting to raise your children? The world, the school system, or this society? Who or what is influencing their lives? Are you doing what God has commanded of us as parents?

In Ephesians 6:1-4 we learn, *"children are to submit to their parents,"* and specifically, <u>fathers</u> are called upon to bring them up *"in the training and admonition of the Lord."* I wonder if the high school kid who exposed himself in the photo had parents who brought him up in the training and admonition of the Lord? If not, is it his fault he didn't know how to act? Was he raised purely by the world around him? If so, shouldn't this world grant him mercy or take some responsibility?

As the scripture says, *"the world hates you"* (John 15:19).

Look at the case of Mr. Weinstein. On the day he was arrested in May 2018, his lawyer issued this statement:

"Mr. Weinstein did not invent the casting couch in Hollywood. And to the extent that there is bad behavior in that industry, that is not what this is about. Bad behavior is not on trial in this case. It's only if you intentionally committed a criminal act, and Mr. Weinstein vigorously denies that."

Listen to my version of his lawyer's plea: *Seriously? You want to charge my client based on his bad sexual behavior? Everyone does this! It is widely known and accepted in this industry. Why are you singling him out? It's not like he robbed a bank or killed someone.*

Too bad Mr. Weinstein's father never taught him that if he chose to live according to the ways of the world, he would one day be devoured by that same world. Fathers, if you're not training your children in the way of the Lord, you're foolishly launching them, unarmored, into a world where the enemy is eager to destroy them.

CHAPTER 7
PLUNDER HIS HOUSE

> *The evidence of conversion is*
> *not a decision card filled out,*
> *it's a life being lived out.*
>
> ~ Paul Washer

In his book *Irresistible: The Rise of Addictive Technology*, Adam Alter begins by mentioning several high-tech industry leaders who restrict or limit the use of technology in their home, especially with their children. One of them was Chris Anderson, the former editor of *Wired* Magazine. He said his children accuse him of being overly concerned about technology, arguing that none of their friends have the same strict rules when it comes to their gadgets. Anderson's response to his strict stance? "We have seen the dangers of technology firsthand. I've seen it in myself. I don't want to see that happen to my kids."

Let me ask a question here. Please know I do so first as a soldier for the Kingdom of God, and second to spur you to fully become the man God intended you to be. What kind of fruit comes from watching TV, scrolling social media, or playing video games for countless hours in your life? In fact, as a secular-dominated industry, it invites strongholds and addictions in your life whether you realize it or not. You think I'm overreacting? Regarding video gaming and social media addictions, there are now rehab centers all over the world trying to reverse the damage being done to both kids and adults. Listen to this: In 2018, the World Health Organization added "gaming disorder" as a new mental illness in their international classification of diseases. One of my biggest frustrations is when a man tells me he struggles with sexual immorality but doesn't see anything wrong with all the movies, games, music, and social media he allows his flesh to ingest every day. This is equivalent to a man who eats junk food every day only to be puzzled by his sudden weight gain.

Have you ever seen those abstract or 3-dimensional pictures that contain a hidden image? Once your eyes spot the hidden image, it suddenly becomes obvious. From that point on you can't look at the picture without seeing it. However, if you don't see the hidden image, all you see is a confused mess. Similarly, a man who allows his flesh to absorb worldly lusts while simultaneously seeking sexual purity, will become a confused mess as well. 1 Corinthians 15:33 states, "*Do not be deceived: Evil company corrupts good habits.*" If you're a man who has fallen victim here, wake up! You're muzzled. Give up everything that comes between you and the Lord. If you're tired of going nowhere, surrender your life to God and unmuzzle yourself from the grip Satan has been using to hold you back. Take inventory of all the "worldly faucets" you allow to drip onto you and your family. Do you allow your TV to spew worldliness and evil into your home? I'm not just talking about rated-R movies. What about the TV shows, commercials, and news you allow to flow into your home? What about the music you allow to penetrate your mind that aims to desensitize your spirit? What social media do you allow your flesh to absorb daily? Ask yourself, "Are these faucets watering my spirit, or poisoning my soul?"

FORGIVEN, BUT UNCONFESSED

I can't tell you how many times I've witnessed a Christian man throw his hands up in complete bewilderment regarding the problems in his marriage or with his children. One specific example is a man I met about ten years ago through my business. We quickly became friends upon discovering several commonalities and interests. Over hundreds of lunches, we shared our lives with each other and grew to become close friends. He was an airline pilot, married, with grown children.

Meeting for lunch one day, my spirit became burdened as I walked toward him. Due to the uncomfortable nature of what I felt about him, more than a year had passed before I gained the courage to bring it up. As our relationship grew, so did the depth of our conversations. One day he randomly told me that his wife didn't always go to church or attend home group with him. He said it was mostly due to her "social anxiety." I also learned both of his adult children had completely fallen away from Christianity, and one was in a homosexual relationship. I asked him what he thought caused his children to stray so far off course from the Christian home they grew up in. I'll never forget him throwing his hands in the air, looking up and saying: "Heaven help me, I have no idea."

I did. He was muzzled. The burden I felt when meeting him for lunch a year prior: He had committed adultery. Matthew 12:29 says: "*Or how can one enter a strong man's house and plunder his goods, unless he first binds the strong man? And then he will plunder his house."* This is Jesus himself speaking to the Pharisees illustrating how He will bind Satan. However, did you know Satan knows God's Word? In fact, it was Satan who quoted Psalm 91:11-12 in an attempt to convince Jesus to throw himself off the temple rooftop (Matthew 4:6). What's my point? Satan is using sexual sin to bind men and plunder homes all over the world.

Unable to shake it was the Holy Spirit who was at work in me to help this man, I gained the courage and confidence to finally approach him. At lunch one day, I said, "I sense you've been unfaithful to your wife." Prepared for him to leave, or worse, punch me in the face, he instead downplayed it as if he already told me. "I told you that, didn't I?" he countered. "No, I definitely would have remembered," I quickly responded. He further downplayed it by

SEXUAL SIN GIVES THE ENEMY JURISDICTION TO COME IN, BIND YOU, AND THEN WREAK HAVOC IN YOUR LIFE.

telling me how common it was in his vocation as an airline pilot. "Does your wife know?" I asked. "No, and she never will," he quickly countered. Wow. I asked if he would consider praying about telling her. "I already did, and God said all is good and I'm forgiven," he enthusiastically responded. Somehow, I found the audacity to ask him to pray again. He hesitantly agreed to do so. A few weeks later, he informed me God confirmed there was no need to tell his wife. "God said it was unnecessary to cause further damage since I've already been forgiven," he said.

Again, it's like those abstract pictures with the hidden image. If you don't see the hidden image, it's a mess of a picture. I believe this is where many men are today. Like my friend, they cannot see that sexual sin has allowed Satan to plunder their home. Sexual sin gives the enemy jurisdiction to come in, bind you, and then wreak havoc in your life.

Many Christians don't see, believe, or obey the instructions, insights, warnings, and biblical directives God gives us. The muzzle prevents them from seeking God and ingesting His Word. Their misuse of grace converts them into a useless wet match, and their sexual sin keeps them bound from fulfilling the role of the spiritual leader in the home. Because they don't act upon God's Word, they don't experience the promised blessings of obedience to it. When a father doesn't or can't (because he's muzzled) truly press into, act on, and believe the Bible (where all the instructions for fathering are found), he is not the father his children desperately need him to be. Unless a course correction is made (for starters...confessing sin), one day he may throw his hands in the air and wonder how his marriage, or his children ended up so far off course.

Like my friend, I believe there are many men who plan to take their "forgiven" but "unconfessed" sin to the grave. Don't misunderstand; I'm not talking about salvation here. Jesus bore our sins on the cross and as true followers of Christ, by His blood, we are forgiven. I'm talking about choosing to tie God's hands from blessing you, your marriage, your children and your legacy. In chapter four, I said if you're not humbly willing to confess all your sins to your spouse, you're choosing to keep God out of your marriage. Ephesians 5:11 tells us, *"And have no fellowship with the unfruitful works of darkness, but rather expose them."* James 5:16 instructs, *"Confess your trespasses to one another, and pray for one another, that you may be healed."* If this describes you, do not be deceived. You may have God's forgiveness and maybe even eternal salvation, but if you trap darkness in your life, you are choosing to shut the door on God. I share this story to awaken you. We live in a world where too many "Christians" compromise and selectively obey God's Word. Don't be one of them.

CHAPTER 8
WHY A MUZZLE?

There are three basic reasons to muzzle a dog:

1. To prevent barking
2. To prevent eating
3. To prevent biting

When you give in to sexual sin, the enemy muzzles you for these same three reasons. When you muzzle a dog, you take away its primary ability to communicate, sustain and protect itself. When the enemy is given jurisdiction to muzzle a believer, it restrains these same abilities between him and his Master,

God Almighty. The Bible tells us in Proverbs 18:21, *"Death and life are in the power of the tongue."* A Christian man struggling with sexual sin walks around with a muzzle strapped across his mouth. He is restrained from receiving God's sustenance and care. He finds it difficult to speak to, interact with, and obey God. Eventually, he begins to believe there is no real point in trying. A muzzled man can't fathom God would hear or even desire to be near him. Why? Because a man in sexual sin shamefully believes God is distant or against him.

BARKING

A sinning man will stop praying; a praying man will stop sinning.

- Leonard Ravenhill

A muzzled man finds great difficulty in talking to God. Like a muzzled dog, he eventually finds a spot, cowers down, and begins to waste the days away. Think about this: Satan would be pleased if Christian men would simply find a spot on this earth, lay down and shut up. He is completely against you "barking." Men who pray and speak God's promises over themselves, their wives, their children...barking. Men who pray and meditate on scripture...barking. Men who ask God for His intercession and help in their lives...barking. Men who praise and worship the Lord...barking. Bottom line: Satan hates men who bark and will pounce at all opportunities to muzzle them. If he can't muzzle them, he will leave. *James 4:7 states, "Therefore submit to God. Resist the devil and he will flee from you."* The enemy cannot remain in the presence of a man "barking" for the Lord.

EATING

I am the living bread which came down from heaven. If anyone eats of this bread, he will live forever; and the bread that I shall give is My flesh, which I shall give for the life of the world.
John 6:51

A muzzled man finds great difficulty consuming the spiritual sustenance in the Bible. Reading or hearing the Word of God doesn't digest well for a believer who has committed sexual sin.

HIDDEN AND HABITUAL SEXUAL SIN IS A HOME RUN FOR THE ENEMY.

It puts him in a state of unworthiness, and he finds it difficult to ingest God's Word. It stings like salt being poured into an open wound. Although a man in sexual sin hungers for what the Word offers, he often just hopelessly stares at it.In the same way a muzzled dog would if a slice of meat was placed in front him.

Incapacitated and with eyes full of despair, he can only gaze at the sustenance he was designed to devour.

It's our wretched habit of tolerating sin that keeps us in our half-dead condition.
~ A.W. Tozer

The muzzle also makes it difficult for men to confess or reach out for help. It's why wives all over the world are dumbfounded and devastated when they find out their Christian husbands have been addicted to porn or have been hiding an affair. It's why a pastor struggling with sexual sin continues in his work instead of rushing himself to the altar. He is ignorant that Satan is leading him to be slaughtered. The muzzle holds him in bondage and shame, restraining him from confession. This pastor, like many Christians today, begins to accept his struggle. Hidden and habitual sexual sins are home runs for the enemy. This grip restrains a man from seeking God and blocks him from receiving all God has for him. If you remain a Christian, but fall away from God and His Word, you will become what the Bible calls *lukewarm*. In Revelation 3:26, God says he will spit you out of His mouth if you end up here: *"So then, because you are lukewarm, and neither cold nor hot, I will vomit you out of My mouth."*

Men, His Word is nourishment to your entire body, soul, mind and spirit. The Word of God is fuel for your spirit! It is the sustenance many men are starving for. Sadly, when your spirit is closed off from receiving God's Word, you will only be left with your flesh to feed and sustain you. God never designed you to thrive in this half-dead condition.

BITING

Deliver those who are drawn toward death, and hold back those stumbling to the slaughter.
Proverbs 24:11

If you muzzle a dog while in the presence of others, it's often to prevent it from biting. Why would the enemy muzzle a man for this reason? Wouldn't this instead be in line with Satan's tactics to hurt others? Yes, if the biting I'm referring to was meant for harm. But remember who Satan aims to muzzle: Christian men. Why would Christians need to be restrained from biting others? In chapter two, I stated sexual sin is a hidden epidemic and proposed every pastor in the world should be sounding the alarm on it. Christians muzzled by sexual sin find it difficult to reprove or, if you will, "bite" others in sexual sin. A muzzled man cannot effectively call out sexual sin, or "grab hold" of others who are struggling. In other words, they have no biting power! Instead, they do their best to nudge or rub against it. Imagine a father who finds out his son is looking at porn but has no ability to call it out or "bite". If he is harnessed by it, how is he supposed to grab his son? This is no different from a pastor in sexual sin. He can only offer a so-called grace with no solution to men who struggle. However, a man without a muzzle is capable of biting. This man can truly take a stance against sexual sin.

I once heard author and evangelist, James Robison, say it this way: "Do you know why so few people get free today? Because it takes free people to free people!" I call these men *Unmuzzled Men*. Their assignment: Grab hold of men heading toward the slaughter.

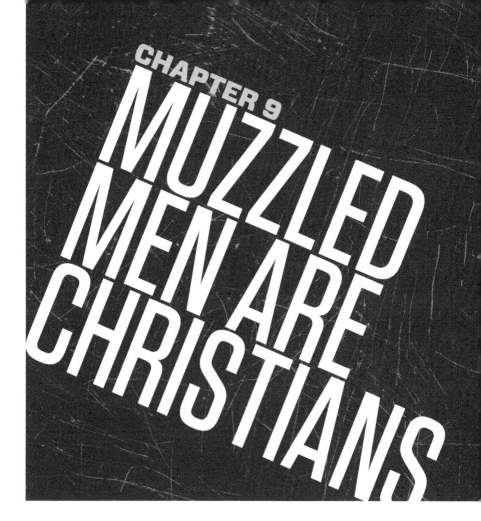

CHAPTER 9

MUZZLED MEN ARE CHRISTIANS

I discipline my body and keep it under control, lest after preaching to others I myself should be disqualified.

1 Corinthians 9:27

If you've been to any marriage seminar or church men's event, you are aware that passivity is often addressed as a common denominator regarding the problem with men today. Listen up: Identify a passive Christian man and you will likely find a man harnessed by sexual sin. According to a national survey conducted over a five-year period by Pure Desire Ministries,

68% of **Christian** men viewed pornography on a regular basis. Furthermore, the vocational pastors sitting on the platform are harnessed as well. A recent study done by Josh McDowell and Barna Research revealed a disastrous 57% of **pastors** and 64% of **youth pastors** are struggling with it.

The first time I remember encountering a muzzled man occurred several years ago when my wife and I were leading a church home group. During group one evening, a wife asked the group for prayer. Notice I said the wife asked, not the husband. This couple had been trying to have a child for quite some time and their doctor recently told them they might not be able to conceive. That night, we surrounded this young couple and cried out for God's intervention in their lives. Afterwards, I spoke with the husband and asked if he was leading as the spiritual leader of his home. I'll never forget the look on his face. Looking at him, I could tell he desired to pray and wished he could tell me he had been, but he hadn't. He could barely mutter a word to even respond to me. As I looked at him, it was as the word *PASSIVE was* written across his forehead. I ended our conversation by declaring God had called him to be the pastor of his home. I encouraged him to pray for his wife's womb and declare God's provision in it.

IDENTIFY A PASSIVE CHRISTIAN MAN AND YOU WILL LIKELY FIND A MAN HARNESSED BY SEXUAL SIN.

About a year later, his wife gave birth to a healthy baby girl. Sometime after this, I was speaking at a men's retreat. This same man came up to me and asked if we could talk privately. He confessed he had struggled with pornography for many years, in fact, throughout his entire marriage. As he talked, I was immediately taken back to that night at home group. I remembered that restrained look on his face as he tried to answer why he wasn't leading and praying as the pastor of the home. He was muzzled.

A man muzzled by sexual sin is a man who finds it difficult to pray, praise, and worship God. Like a muzzled dog, he begins to accept his condition and slowly stops fighting it. Today, I encounter muzzled men everywhere. This is especially true inside the church. Muzzled men are either Christians or on the path to becoming Christians. Think about it. The non-believer engaged in sexual immorality isn't seeking, worshiping, or praying. Why would Satan need to muzzle them? In the rhetorical spirit of the late evangelist David Wilkerson, *he'd be a stupid devil to muzzle a dead dog!*

Once you become free from sexual sin and recognize this scheme of the enemy, you too will spot other muzzled men. The emptiness in their spirit often reveals the muzzle across their mouth. Much like the emptiness you might see in the eyes of a muzzled dog lying flat on the ground, staring at that slice of meat he finally gave up fighting to devour. Even though God is right in front of him, a muzzled man feels fully restricted from accessing Him.

It's an overwhelming burden to see and it is the driving force behind this entire message. I encounter muzzled men nearly every day. It's a constant battle of discernment of whether I am making an assumption on a man, or if it's the Holy Spirit revealing it. So, I do the only thing I know to do. If I have the opportunity to approach a man I sense is muzzled, I *bite*. *"Hey, do you struggle with pornography?"* or *"Hey, do you have hidden sexual sin in your life?"* I ask. Overwhelmingly, the answer is yes. If they allow, I explain how it was their muzzle that gave it away to me. Now, as you might suspect, this ignites conversations! More times than not, I'll witness muzzled men walk away unmuzzled.

Now, several men I've encountered would immediately answer, "No. I'm a Christian." If these men allowed me to continue talking with them, the overwhelming majority would finally confess their struggle. There are a growing number of Christians who justify this sin and somehow believe they're exempt from having to admit it. Many years ago, I asked a client who was a personal fitness trainer who often worked with females, how he withstood the "fire" that surrounded him in his job. His response: "I'm a Christian and I love my wife." About three years later, he and his wife came in for another vehicle purchase. After catching up for just a few seconds, I instantly could see he was muzzled. Weeks later when he came back to the office (this time without his wife), I *bit* and asked him if he was in sexual sin. Not only

SATAN CELEBRATES CHRISTIANS WHO HIDE AND JUSTIFY SEXUAL SIN.

did he admit to struggling with pornography since childhood, he confessed to having multiple affairs over the years. Satan celebrates Christians who hide and justify sexual sin. News flash: You can't hide from God.

For My eyes are on all their ways; they are not hidden from My face, nor is their iniquity hidden from My eyes.
Jeremiah 16:17

"Can anyone hide himself in secret places, So I shall not see him?"
says the Lord; "Do I not fill heaven and earth?" says the Lord.
Jeremiah 23:24

Has sexual sin muzzled you and rendered you useless for the Kingdom of God? Are you a muzzled husband who is not fulfilling the headship role God intends for you? Are you a muzzled father whose children are deprived of prayer, words of affection, wisdom, and training that is supposed to come from you? Are you a muzzled Christian who is half-dead because you're not feeding your spirit with the Word of God?

God created you with purpose and value for His kingdom. Satan is fully aware of the dividends it pays to muzzle just one man. When he can shut you up and hold you back from becoming the man God called you to be, it impacts your marriage, your children, and your ministry. In his book, *The Noticer*, Andy Andrews makes this powerful statement: "There are generations yet unborn, whose very lives will be shifted and shaped by the moves and the actions you take." Wake up men of God! Do not allow the enemy to ransack your home. Research now shows the average child is exposed to pornography somewhere between 8 and 9 years of age. This has been going on for decades. A journal article, "*The Nature and Dynamics of Internet Pornography Exposure for Youth*," reported 93% of boys and 62% of girls are exposed to Internet porn before they are 18 years old. That was in 2008! Today, it's likely that 99% of children will be exposed to porn by the time they are 18. Fathers, if you are not the gatekeeper of your home, the enemy will gladly step in for you. If you're giving in to sexual sin of any kind, the enemy has you muzzled down in the corner of your home, while wreaking havoc in your marriage and children. Equally as bad, if you're not yet married or are without children, the enemy is dumping poison on the fruit God has prepared for you as a husband or father-to-be.

What father would willingly open the door and allow someone to come in and rip the innocence from his son or daughter? In a poll by *Focus on the Family*, 47% of Christian families said pornography was a problem in their home. That was way back in 2003! A recent publication by Josh McDowell Ministries reported that 91% of children now find pornography when they're not even searching for it. Fathers, we are accountable to the Lord as the gatekeepers of our homes. *"But if anyone does not provide for his own, and especially for those of his household, he has denied the faith and is worse than an unbeliever"* (1 Timothy 5:8).

If you're struggling with sexual sin, the enemy's goal is to make you a powerless pastor and a passive husband and father. Have you ever seen the enemy's attack from this angle? If he can keep you in bondage, not only can he destroy you, he's given access to your wife and children. How? Because you are muzzled. *"Or how can one enter a strong man's house and plunder his goods, unless he first binds the strong man? And then he will plunder his house"* (Matthew 12:29). As I said in chapter seven, I believe Satan has adopted this scripture and is using sexual sin to bind men from fulfilling the role of pastor or the

WE ARE DANGEROUSLY CONSTRUCTING AN ALL-ENCOMPASSING CHRISTIAN CULTURE THAT DELETE CHUNKS OF THE BIBLE IT DEEMS OUTDATED OR IRRELEVANT FOR TODAY'S SOCIETY.

spiritual leader in their homes. Furthermore, if you're a vocational pastor or church leader bound by sexual sin, could this mean you're giving Satan access to plunder your church? A muzzled pastor eventually learns to praise, worship, and teach right through his muzzle. Desensitized by his sin and often soaked in "cheap grace," he is a wet match. He looks like a pastor, acts like a pastor, but at his core, he's a dud. If this is you, I'm not trying to offend your flesh, I'm trying to ignite your spirit.

As previously stated, this is a serious epidemic in the church today. How can a muzzled pastor lead his flock? It is one of the primary reasons we are producing Christians who believe they can accept and reject parts of the Bible as they see fit. We are dangerously constructing an all-encompassing Christian culture that delete chunks of the Bible it deems outdated or irrelevant for today's society. Instead of spreading the entire Word of God, we have pastors today, using so-called grace to extinguish scriptures that rub people too harshly. Today, this has produced "Christians" you'd have a tough time picking out in a club full of idolaters.

If you are a muzzled Christian, the enemy has laughingly branded you a passive dud to God. This is no longer some struggle or problem we face, it's a full-scale invasion. Today, most Christian men I meet with are struggling with sexual sin. The purpose of this book is two-fold. First, to ignite a fire inside you to recognize the enemy's attack. Second, to reveal what God's Word has instructed you to do as the Kingdom warrior He created you to be. God is chasing you to turn you around from the slaughter the enemy is leading you toward. Sexual sin is one tiny dart capable of destroying a man's entire life purpose.

CHAPTER 10

SATAN'S NUMBER ONE TARGET

For she has cast down many wounded, and all who were slain by her were strong men.

Proverbs 7:26

David, Samson, and Solomon were all strong men who were anointed and called by God to do great things. Yet, all three of them had disastrous sexual sin in their lives. The consequences they each faced were catastrophic. Samson lost his eyes, David lost a son, and Solomon lost his faith in God. In Numbers 22-25, we read of when the Israelites were camped in the plains of

Moab, near Jericho, in route to their promised land. The ruler of the region, King Balak, feared the Israelites would overtake them like they did the Amorites before. Terrified, the King called upon and paid the prophet Balaam to ask God to remove them. After several attempts, God rejected Balaam's call and instead increased His blessings on the Israelites. Realizing God was not going to do anything, they devised a plan to turn the Israelites against God. Their strategy? The King instructed his women to entice the Israelite men with sex if they bowed and worshipped Baal. Boom. Sexual temptation instantly crumbled these once strong and God-fearing men. The cost? God ordered Moses to kill all who participated.

SEXUAL SIN IS NOT JUST SOMETHING YOU MUST REPENT OF, IT'S SOMETHING YOU MUST OBLITERATE FROM YOUR LIFE.

Like Samson, David, Solomon, and the Israelite men in Moab, we are all susceptible to this incapacitating sin. It can cause you to walk right off a cliff even while knowing the severe consequences that will follow.

Several years ago, internationally known Christian apologist and Bible teacher, Ravi Zacharias was accused of sexual harassment by a married woman whom he had been counseling. He and his organization immediately denied the claim and even filed a lawsuit against the woman for extortion. Following Ravi's unexpected death in 2020, three additional women came forward and accused Ravi of sexual abuse spanning more than a decade.

Ravi Zacharias International Ministries was appalled and immediately dismissed the claims, denied the allegations, and confidently defended their leader by hiring an independent investigative firm to debunk the accusations.

A few months into the investigation, enough evidence was brought forth that caused the ministry to instantly concede and admit defeat. That evidence confirmed the widely known and celebrated Christian apologist, Ravi Zacharias, sexually harassed, manipulated and engaged in physical sexual acts with multiple women.

I highly recommend John Piper's commentary regarding the fall of Ravi Zacharias. I'll entice you with his closing statement:

"The last thing I would say to those who came to Christ under Ravi's ministry, or who had their faith mightily strengthened by what he taught, is this: Don't let the imperfections and failures of men turn you away from the perfections and the triumphs of Christ, who will never, never fail you. - John Piper

Men, I am sounding an alarm that should be ringing loudly in every Bible-based church in the world! That alarm is simply this: we are ALL at risk of falling flat on our face into sexual sin. It doesn't matter who you are, your status in the church or how many times you've read the Bible! It doesn't matter whether you're a new Christian or have been one for 70 years. And it definitely doesn't matter if you are a pastor or in vocational ministry.

As a Christ-follower, you are not immune to sexual temptation, you are Satan's number one target for it.

CHAPTER 11

FIREPROOF

...able to withstand fire or great heat
- English-Oxford Dictionary

Remember Rand McNally? Twenty years ago if you were headed out on a road trip, you would need to purchase a physical map, typically a *Rand McNally Road Atlas*. They were at the front of every Wal-Mart and convenience store on the planet. Today, we all have access to that map whenever we want. Once you tell your phone or navigation device where you want to go, it immediately gives you the most efficient route. Gone are the days of giant atlas books you'd find between the seats of nearly every car. The same can be said for pornography. Years ago, you had to make an effort to find it. You had to go somewhere off the beaten path to purchase a magazine or a video. Today, it's free and sadly most of us are desensitized to it. Sexual temptation is everywhere. Even if you're not looking for it, it's looking for you.

Today, sex is big business. Sexual temptation is forced into your daily life, and the enticement of it should be illegal. However, not only is it legal, this world is flooded with it. Recently, I was researching the real estate market and mortgage interest rates for my parents, who were looking to refinance their home. I'd been reading articles about mortgage rates and gathering information for them. As I began to scroll through an article, a picture and caption caught my eye from the right column. The picture was a scantily-dressed woman in a seductive pose with the caption, "Best way to do a cash-out refinance." *You've got to be kidding,* I said to myself. This world is absolutely against your purity. Remember the arcade game at the Bass Pro Shop I spoke of in chapter six? Do not be deceived. The use of sex in advertising has become an epidemic and sexual sin is Satan's number one weapon of choice on men.

The goal of online market research today is to identify where your next click or purchase will be. It studies you in real-time. It's called "programmatic advertising" or "behavioral marketing." Self-learning algorithms quickly collect your tastes and tendencies to dispense the most effective bait needed to hook you. Did you search the latest football scores, schedules, or stats? *Well, there is a good chance this is a male,* conclude the behind-the-scenes data crawlers. Or, maybe you're searching cars, perhaps a luxury sport sedan. *There's a good chance this is a married male in his 30's who has young children,* conclude the data crawlers. The search algorithm silently predicts: *The wife has an SUV and he wants something that can carry the kids in case he needs to, but still have something sporty and fun to drive. I bet he would bite on an image of a provocatively dressed supermodel. Cast the lure and let's try to hook him.*

Remember: The world isn't leading you to Heaven, it's pushing you to Hell. Men, you can be doing your best to be all you can be for God, your wife, and your children; but completely unaware the enemy is up ahead of you with a plan to knock you off course. If you're a married man, the enemy would love nothing more than to cause you to crash. Why? A divorce is a grand slam for the enemy. It destroys you, your wife, your children, and often produces generational curses and iniquities. Marriage is a commonly sought-after prize for Satan.

SEXUAL SIN, PAST OR PRESENT, ALWAYS POISONS A MARRIAGE.

If you're not yet married, *even better*, the enemy roars. *Let's get him entangled before he is married! It will only make it easier to take him down once he is.* A man who is sexually active or experimenting sexually prior to marriage is sabotaging his future. Nearly all the single men I meet with who struggle with sexual purity tend to disagree with this assessment. They usually counter argue with their plan to be pure once married. However, the consequences of sexual immorality usually don't manifest until a man marries. Then they appear and wreak havoc. Why would the Bible constantly warn against it if there were no real consequences? Ask a few men who have carried sexual sin into a marriage if they would have done things differently. Sexual sin, past or present, *always* poisons a marriage.

My son, pay attention to my wisdom; listen carefully to my wise counsel. Then you will show discernment, and your lips will express what you've learned. For the lips of an immoral woman are as sweet as honey, and her mouth is smoother than oil. But in the end she is as bitter as poison, as dangerous as a double-edged sword. Her feet go down to death; her steps lead straight to the grave.
Proverbs 5:1-5, NLT

The enemy doesn't have a mercy mode, and his endgame is simple: steal, kill and destroy. Picture those spike strips the police use to stop a vehicle they've been chasing. The police anticipate where a vehicle is headed and then lay down the spikes to blow out its tires. The enemy does the same with sexual sin, and he targets Christians. He is down the road, setting out spikes in anticipation of you passing by. Men, we must not only be purposeful, but vigilant about staying away from all forms of sexual temptation.

Here are 10 examples of Christian men who have run through Satan's spike strips:

1. Men who have pre-marital sex or engage in affairs during marriage.
2. Men who say music, movies, video games, or social media with sexual content don't affect them.
3. Married men who don't see anything wrong with having relationships or going to lunch alone with other females.
4. Men who tolerate sexual banter with their buddies.
5. Married men who have separate female friends outside of their marriage.
6. Men who go to sensually themed restaurants or clubs.
7. Men who lie when confronted about sexual sin.
8. Men who believe looking at porn, flirting or lustful thoughts are innocent as long as they don't physically engage.

9. Men who believe sex is a physical need and thereby justify sinful behavior.

1 Peter 5:8 warns, "Be sober, be vigilant; because your adversary the devil walks about like a roaring lion, seeking whom he may devour." This is a healthy warning that brings a keen sense of awareness that the enemy is after us. It's critical we open our spiritual eyes, resist the enemy, and stay away from all sexual immorality. God has given the Word to avoid sin, not a so-called grace to excuse us of it.

GOD HAS GIVEN THE WORD TO AVOID SIN, NOT A SO-CALLED GRACE TO EXCUSE US OF IT.

THE FLESH IS FLAMMABLE

...above all, taking the shield of faith with which you will be able to quench all the fiery darts of the wicked one.
Ephesians 6:16

Once you're hit with a *fiery dart* of sexual temptation, a lustful residue infiltrates your flesh, and you can quickly catch on fire. Lust thirsts infinitely and is never quenched. Sadly, like a literal burn, sexual sin often leaves a lasting scar. It's a sin like all sins in that it never satisfies. But remember, unlike all other sins, the Bible tells us sexual sin is unique and in a category all its own:

"Flee sexual immorality. Every sin that a man does is outside the body, but he who commits sexual immorality <u>sins against his own body</u>" (1 Corinthians 6:18).

Today, there seems to be an endless stream of sexual temptation darts flying. It's no longer a single shot fired here and there, it's an all-out assault. In fact, pornography is now everywhere. We have gone from a society once quietly appalled by pornography to a society loudly applauding it. The enemy knows if he hits you with this dart, the only way you will recover is if you invite God to intervene. The only way God intervenes is if you ask Him to.

WE HAVE GONE FROM A SOCIETY ONCE QUIETLY APPALLED BY PORNOGRAPHY TO A SOCIETY LOUDLY APPLAUDING IT.

For *"whoever calls on the name of the Lord shall be saved."*
Romans 10:13

The only way you will ever call on Him is if you truly believe He is for you and His love is everlasting–even in the shame of sexual sin.

If God is for us, who can be against us?
Romans 8:31

The only way to truly believe this passage is to let go of shame and completely surrender to God.

He who did not spare His own Son, but delivered Him up for us all, how shall He not with Him also freely give us all things?
Romans 8:32

But wait! If you do this, isn't that admitting defeat and giving up? Yes, it is. Men who won't admit their struggles and ask God for help are as stubborn and ignorant as men who get lost because they refuse to stop and ask for directions. Is it possible the enemy has figured out how to use this to his advantage? Here is the enemy's attack strategy: 1) *Incapacitate them with sexual sin.* 2) *Apply muzzle.* 3) *Convince them to conceal regret and shame with "grace" and passivity.*

Once he has you there, he doesn't stop. It is not enough for the enemy just to keep you silent and passive. This is only the beginning for him. He will lead you down a path of complete destruction.

A prudent man foresees evil and hides himself, But the simple pass on and are punished.
Proverbs 22:3

The most common rebuttals I hear when challenging men to make drastic changes in their lives are: *"I'm good. I'm not that weak. I'm over that. I've been set free."* They believe they have somehow arrived and don't need to safeguard themselves from what they consider "normal" activities and situations. A man who believes he can stand strong in the heat of sexual temptation is as foolish as a man who believes he can casually stroll through a blazing inferno and emerge unburned. In case you haven't caught it yet, the flesh is flammable.

Men often think: *I can withstand. I can look and not touch. I'm strong enough to resist.* Christian men will literally ask God to help them not fall into temptation as they enter venues full of temptation. *Lord, give me eyes for my wife only.* Asking God to supernaturally manipulate your physical eyes is not the solution. *Forgive me Father for lusting while watching that movie. Help me to be stronger next time.* How about not watching any more movies with sexual immorality? Men, it's time

WHEN YOU ALLOW YOUR FLESH TO BE SEXUALLY TEMPTED, YOU INCAPACITATE YOUR ABILITY TO RESIST IT.

to realize it's not about your inability to resist sexual fires, it's about recognizing you're not fireproof! No software protection, accountability or counseling will ever change the flesh. Quit believing you can take fire! Yes, you are that weak, the Bible says so. When you allow your flesh to be sexually tempted, you incapacitate your ability to resist it. You're not fireproof.

CHAPTER 12
SIN NEVER SATISFIES

Sin always takes you farther than you want to go, keeps you longer than you want to stay, and costs you more than you are willing to pay.

- Ravi Zacharias

I began this book with a story about a thirty-six-year-old Christian husband and father of three young children. As he wrote from prison, he admitted he couldn't fathom what he had done. It all began with a "harmless" addiction to pornography. Today, if you were to search for it, you'd quickly discover there are thousands, maybe tens of thousands of men sitting in prison for the same exact reason. Many of them profess to be Christians like my NSX friend. The Bible warns us: *"Hell and Destruction are never full; So the eyes of man are never satisfied"* (Proverbs 27:20). Have you ever thought about how this relates to sexual sin? It means sexual sin will continue to take you deeper and deeper into it.

Men, the enemy is not satisfied merely to keep you muzzled. His intent is to one day destroy you. You may read this and conclude my NSX friend was a sick and demented person–and you would be justified to think so. In the book, *The Brain That Changes Itself*, it shows pornography has the same damaging effects on the brain as drugs such as cocaine or heroin. In other words, it messes you up. This guy started out viewing general adult pornography. But over the years, he began sinking deeper into it. Eventually, the enemy had him exactly where he needed him. This guy lost his wife, his children, and his life as he

PORNOGRAPHY HAS THE SAME DAMAGING EFFECTS ON THE BRAIN AS DRUGS SUCH AS COCAINE OR HEROIN.

knew it. The moment he began viewing pornography was the moment he invited Satan to lead him to the slaughter.

I mentioned Ted Bundy in chapter six, but it's appropriate to bring him up again here. If you have never watched Dr. James Dobson's interview with Ted Bundy, I recommend it. The night before he was to be executed for the rape and murder of more than thirty women and children, Bundy requested to be interviewed by Dr. Dobson. He stated he chose Dr. Dobson because he knew he could trust him to clearly relay the message he wanted to share with the world. Read the following excerpt from the interview:

"I grew up in a wonderful home where we regularly attended church with two Christian parents. Basically, I was a normal person. I'm not blaming pornography for my actions, but that is where it started. I'm here to send a warning because I don't want there to be any more Ted Bundys created. I've lived in prison a long time now. I've met a lot of men who were motivated to commit violence just like me. And without exception, every one of them was deeply involved in pornography."

Sadly, we live in a world that completely discredited his admissions. The world condemned him for blaming his unimaginable crimes on something as "harmless" as pornography. You would think if a man who was sentenced to death for more than thirty rapes, mutilations, and murders told the world it was rooted in pornography, something drastic would have been done about it. Instead, the world has done more to advance the availability, accessibility, and acceptance of pornography.

Reason Magazine ran this headline in August 2016: *"The FBI Distributes Child Pornography to Catch People Who Look at It."* Think about this tactic for a minute. *Instead of working to eradicate this stuff and protect our society from it, let's instead entice people with it. Then we can take them down.* The FBI's goal: Bait the "bad" guys and protect society. The enemy's goal: Destroy men. Don't misunderstand me, I want these men to go to prison. I think it's their last wake-up call before they physically hurt women or children. However, I don't want any more of us to end up there. When it comes to sin, the world is the exact opposite of the Kingdom of God. Nowhere in the Bible does it say Satan is fair and just. In fact, it tells us the exact opposite: *"Satan is the accuser of the brethren"* (Revelation 12:10). Men, when you enter into sexual sin on the internet, you may believe it's your own private playhouse; but you're actually walking into Satan's courthouse.

There is no doubt in my mind that my NSX friend ever fathomed the unthinkable desire for child pornography in his initial encounters with porn. In the extreme case of Ted Bundy, he looks and talks just like you and me in his interview with Dr. Dobson. In fact, throw a sport coat on him, introduce him as a pastor, and you wouldn't think anything differently. Satan's singular goal is to destroy God's plan for your life.

Therefore let him who thinks he stands take heed lest he fall.
1 Corinthians 10:12

This verse is a direct warning. Your struggle may not be to the extreme level of Bundy or my NSX friend, and I'm thankful if it's not. However, do not be deceived. If you read these stories and believe your sin is innocent compared to these guys, you're deceived. Again, 1 Peter 5:8 says, *"Be sober, be vigilant; because your adversary the devil walks about like a roaring lion, seeking whom he may devour."* If you allow the enemy to come in, his end game is to destroy. Whether it's a lustful thought, a mental fantasy, or occasionally looking at porn, all sexual immorality gives Satan access to plunder your life. Please catch this: Your front door may be locked, but sexual sin gives Satan access to the back door.

I see many Christians today straddling the gates of Hell in sexual sin. They have one foot in Hell and one foot in Heaven. Their actions are nowhere near the level of a Ted Bundy or the NSX guy, but more disguised like Ravi Zacharias. They live like Christians, act like Christians, and even pray and worship like Christians. Sure, they may fall to lustful thoughts, pornography or even sex outside of marriage; but they repent and ask for

God's forgiveness. Sometime later, they find themselves right back in it again. I call this riding the *Grace Train.* The enemy quietly stands aside as you ride this train until you begin to believe it's normal. He calmly waits for you to become a frequent passenger. He doesn't want to push too hard too soon. Instead, he studies and keeps tabs on you. Once you've justified sin, he begins nudging and enticing you to go a little bit further. It's a desensitizing process, and most of the time, you are blind to it. Then, when the timing is right, he'll pounce and claim a victory.

For a righteous man may fall seven times, and rise again, but the wicked shall fall by calamity.
Proverbs 24:16

I don't believe a man who decides to accept and follow Jesus ever purposes to be wicked. If he becomes so, he quickly desires to turn from evil and repent. However, if the cycle of sexual immorality becomes too common to him, he loses his sense of urgency to be rid of it. Hebrews 10:26 states: *For if we sin willfully after we have received the knowledge of the truth, there no longer remains a sacrifice for sins.* I relate this to Jim Rohn's *Law of Diminishing Intent*, which essentially states: *The longer you wait to do something that seems vital and timely, the less likely it is you will ever do it at all.* At some point in your struggle against sexual immorality, your emotions and disgust were on full throttle in opposition to it. You genuinely desired to draw near to God and be freed from it. Did you, or didn't you? If you didn't, was it guilt, shame, fear, or pride that kept you from doing so? Whatever it was, it wasn't from the Lord. He is for you and always offering to draw you near to Him—always (Romans 8:38-39). He created us to run to Him in our struggle.

What is it about sin that keeps us away from the very source that will help us avoid it? John Bunyan, author of the renowned classic *Pilgrims Progress*, wrote this on the inside cover of his personal Bible: "Sin will keep you from this book, or this book will keep you from sin." This is exactly why a muzzled man finds it difficult to ingest the Word of God. Let that soak in for a bit. I once heard author and speaker, Dudley Hall, share a word picture that clearly demonstrates the wrong and the right way to see God:

Religion: *"I've messed up. My dad is going to kill me."*
Son-ship: *"I've messed up. I'd better call my dad."*

As His sons, God will chase after us as long as we walk on this earth. He designed us to be victorious and He is always attempting to reach us, equip us, and lead us to victory. Recognizing and destroying your muzzle removes the restraint holding you from all He has called you to be.

The gift of sonship to God becomes ours not through being born, but through being born again.
~ J.I. Packer

Which man are you?

Are you already that unmuzzled man who is the spiritual leader of your home? If so, please complete this book. This book contains revelation meant to ignite you to become a man God can use to grab others heading toward a slaughter.

Are you the muzzled man whose face contains a shadow of shame (Psalm 34:5)? A man who is remorseful of sin and desperately desires to be freed yet continues to be restrained by it. God didn't create you to be a muzzled dog on a chain like the enemy wants you to believe. You may have shelter, food, and even have some distance to roam, but God isn't satisfied. He created you for a divine purpose. I encourage you to press deeply into this book with humility. There is supernatural freedom and power ahead.

Or are you the man I've labeled a *wet match*? A man who once carried remorse for sin but now simply copes with sin. One who would say God's grace erases and replaces the outdated scriptures and commandments of yesterday. If you're this man, it's likely this book has already offended you. Please hear me. I would not waste my time or energy to offend you. Instead, I challenge you to complete this book. I believe there is transformational grace available to you in this message.

Are you ready to receive God's biblical directives?

Are you prepared to surrender and allow God to enter all areas of your life?

If you are, keep reading. The next section fuels the freedom and hope our spirits desperately desire. You can walk this earth sexually pure and become all God created you to be.

PART 2
GOD'S BIBLICAL DIRECTIVE

CHAPTER 13

S.A.F.E.

It takes a whole Bible to make a whole Christian.

~ Alistair Begg

As I've talked to men over the years, they've shared the tactics and strategies they've been taught on how to "finally get free" from sexual immorality. I thought it would be fitting to share some of them before we see what the Bible actually says. The italicized portions are my own sarcastic comments. Forgive me, I couldn't resist.

→ **Get an accountability partner.** *Once you're accountable, your desire to look will eventually go away after you confess 1,000 times or so.*

→ **Single men: Get married!** *Once married, all your sexual desire will now be perfectly contained.*

→ **Married men: Ask your wife for more sex!** *It's hard to make fun of this one.*

→ **Stop worrying about it. God designed you this way. Fight the good fight and rely on God's unending grace to excuse your shortcomings.** *Go buy a lifetime pass on the Grace Train. All aboard.*

→ **Get supernaturally healed from it.** *Yep, apparently there are men who have managed to grow temptation-proof flesh. These men claim they can look at a naked supermodel without any lust arising in them.*

→ **Get Internet software protection.** *Once you have an Internet filter, your problems will disappear! I think Internet sin blockers are mentioned in the NATB version. You know: The New Age Tech Bible.*

→ **Join a group to understand why pornography is addictive.** *Yep! Once you understand how it messes with your brain, you'll somehow never desire it again!*

→ **Accept the struggle and overcompensate in all other areas of your faith.** *If you continue to do enough religious stuff, it should cover for the areas where you fall short. Definitely keep tithing, volunteering and serving.*

Okay, all my sarcasm aside, anything and everything we can do to *stay away* from sexual temptation *is* part of the equation. Furthermore, it is neither my heart nor my intention to put down anyone who has put forth material meant to rid sexual immorality from people's lives. In fact, I genuinely applaud every person who has taken a stance against sexual sin. However, the message of this book will show you how to go from relying on self-help "tactics" to relying on the original biblical instructions from a supernatural God. Today's tactics tell us freedom from sexual temptation comes from our ability to withstand it. Jesus tells us the opposite. He informs us we are weak and need the help of the Spirit: *"Watch and pray, lest you enter into temptation. The spirit indeed is willing, but the flesh is weak"* (Matthew 26:41).

Several years ago, a customer was in route to my office for an appointment when he texted, *I'm going to be about 20 minutes late. I had to stop for a quick charge.* At the time, his fully electric Nissan Leaf could only go about 100 miles before needing to be recharged. Okay, so here's a silly analogy, but it *drives* the point home! What if there was a "holy charging station" that could revive the Holy Spirit within us? I think many believers who need

GOD WANTS US TO WIN, NOT BARELY CROSS THE FINISH LINE ON FUMES BECAUSE WE "FLESHED" THROUGH THIS LIFE.

to stop and recharge would simply pass by it. You see, unlike a fully electric vehicle that will no longer function once depleted, we function more like hybrids, as flesh and spirit. If we drop in *spirit* power, we switch over to *flesh* power. Technically, we could live this way until we die. However, it's not God's plan for us. He designed us to need Him. In the arena of sexual immorality, men are losing the battle because they're only operating out of their flesh. If you gather the teachings, books, and the latest methods for dealing with lust, pornography, and sexual temptation, you will find most conclude like this: It's a battle, fight the good fight, retrain your eyes, get accountability, will-power through it, pray for healing, and get software protection.

What we're being told is freedom from sexual temptation and sin is found in finding a way for our flesh to resist or fight against it. However, the bible tells us the exact opposite: "*For if you live according to the flesh you will die; but if by the Spirit you put to death the deeds of the body, you will live*" (Romans 8:13). No matter how strong you are or how many layers of protection you have, the flesh is never going to be fireproof against the fiery darts of sexual temptation.

God wants us to win, not barely cross the finish line on fumes because we "fleshed" through this life. The Bible is the spoken and living Word of God. Nothing can be added to it or taken from it. Ecclesiastes 1:9 tells us, "*Nothing new is added under the sun.*" Through His already-spoken word, God laid out the directives for sexual freedom and purity. Proverbs 3:13 states, "*Happy is the man who finds wisdom.*" Most men today believe God is against them in this area of their life. God wants to show you the exact opposite is true. Romans 8:31 says, "*If God is for you, then who can be against you?*"

Men, God is desperately attempting to correct the course of those heading toward a slaughter. Get ready to drop Hell's most celebrated sin: Sexual sin. This muzzling grip is hell-bent on preventing you from reaching God's appointed destiny for your life. The following illustration is your visual guide as you proceed from this point on.

S.A.F.E.

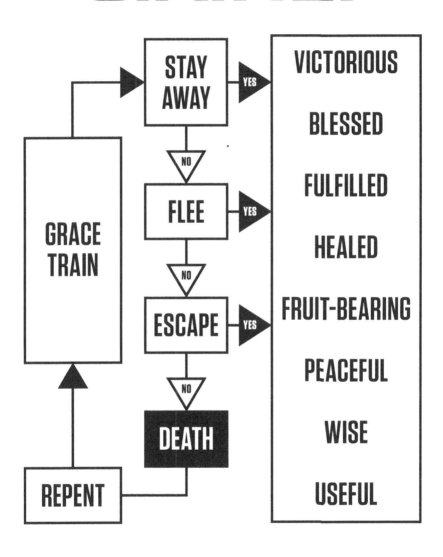

CHAPTER 14
SAWDUST

Did you know a typical table saw blade spins around 4,000 RPM?

My grandfather was a woodworker who converted his garage into a workshop outfitted with all the typical woodworking machinery. I was the only male grandchild in the family and often got to stay the night with him. Not knowing it at the time, my grandfather desperately wanted to do his part to help raise me to succeed as a man. Without any explanation, he one day decided he would call me "Man." That was my name from the time I started walking to the day I led him to rededicate his life to

God before he died. Looking back, whether it was his purpose or not, he was proclaiming manhood over me.

Often, I'd be right there beside him in the workshop. With a section of wood in hand and heading toward the table saw, he would yell out: "Now, Man, stay away! I can't see you coming, and this blade will chew you up and spit you out," as he pointed to the pile of sawdust and wood chips lying all over the ground. Sometimes, a piece of wood would go flying off the table as he fed it through the blade. Other times, the blade would snag on a knot in the wood and send a jolt through my grandfather. Needless to say, I quickly developed a healthy fear of table saws and never disobeyed my grandfather's command to "*stay away.*"

Many years later, during my second year of college, those memories flooded my mind as I was praying for forgiveness of my sexual sins. Except this time, I saw a different scene play out. I found myself believing I could outsmart that spinning blade by feathering my finger across its jagged edge. My spirit whispered: "*You truly believe you can skim the top of that blade and walk away, don't you? You think, worst case, you'll get a minor cut on the tip of your finger? But what you don't realize is every time you head toward the blade; it pulls you through and spits you out on the other side.*" As I opened my eyes, sitting in my apartment, I believed it was the Holy Spirit reminding me of that scene. He knew I was deceived by thinking I could look at women lustfully, view pornography, have mental fantasies, and come away unscathed with just a small prayer for forgiveness. Back then, I often misused grace to excuse my behavior instead of allowing it to transform me. That day I was able to see the deception I was under by believing I could touch the tip of the blade and simply walk away. Instead, I would lose control, become hooked, and then pulled through. Disgusted and destroyed on the other side, my only hope was to repent and ask the Lord for His mercy and grace. I would slowly pull myself up and get on the *Grace Train.* After several days, or sometimes several weeks, I would accept God had forgiven me, exit the train and begin to walk in freedom again.

Like most Christian men I encounter today, if you had caught me after I exited the train and asked if I looked at pornography, I would have said, "I used to, but I've been set free." But, also like most men, I would fall again and be right back on the *Grace Train* countless times more. By His grace and through the blood of Jesus Christ, if you're still breathing, you can repent and be forgiven.

Then, when desire has conceived, it gives birth to sin; and sin, when it is full-grown, brings forth death.
James 1:15

When you land in the box labeled *death* outlined in the s.a.f.e. diagram, the only way back to life is to repent and accept God's grace. However, the enemy is constantly fine-tuning his strategy to keep you in the death box. I think my nsx friend, who now sits in prison, landed in that death box one day fully expecting to repent and go on with his life. This guy had been riding the *Grace Train* for years. It has been nine years since his wife and children watched the FBI escort him away in handcuffs. His life was destroyed by the blade he once believed he could simply touch and walk away from. After all, he had previously walked away from it hundreds of times, seemingly unscathed. He had no idea that one day he wouldn't escape the death box he had bounced out of so many times before. Sitting in his office, filled with guilt, but sunk in his fleshly desire, he found himself drawn to a type of pornography he never could have fathomed. I bet it never crossed his mind the FBI would be knocking at his door that night.

If the enemy comes to steal, to kill, and to destroy, you must start believing that one day, if you continue to leave the door open, he will come for you. In the mid-1600s, John Owen said it best in his book, The Mortification of Sin: *"Be killing sin, or sin will be killing you."* With no parole in sight, my NSX friend is like sawdust, slowly fading away in the minds of the four people he'd give everything to get back. With one timely shot, the enemy destroyed his life. His wife and children will carry this wound for the rest of their lives.

KILL SIN OR IT WILL KILL YOU.

The next section unfolds three biblical instructions. *Stay Away, Flee and Escape* shine a spotlight on God's directives to overcome sexual sin. S.A.F.E. is the primary purpose of this book. It's a biblical sword meant to sever the straps of Satan's muzzle.

CHAPTER 15 STAY AWAY

*Can a man take fire to his bosom,
and his clothes not be burned?
Can one walk on hot coals, and
his feet not be seared?*

Proverbs 6:27-28

To this day, every time I hear a table saw power up, I hear my grandfather grunt, *"Man, stay away."* I believed him, and I stayed away–usually far away. The day I linked together the s.a.f.e. directives, I remember being amazed by how suddenly the scriptures began to form a biblical sword against Satan's scheme.

My grandfather and grandmother ended up divorcing when I was very young. Since I never had the opportunity to know my father's parents, they were my only grandparents. Looking back with the knowledge scripture has revealed to me regarding the severity of sexual sin, I realize it was a huge score for Satan when my grandfather left my grandmother for another woman. The hardship a divorce brings, especially to children, is a lifelong thievery from the enemy. I loved my grandparents dearly. Having them together would have been an amazing gift. Instead, they both remarried, and it was always a battle to enjoy time with either of them.

At Christmas we always went to my grandmother's house. She had a pool–and it was the only pool in the entire town! Not really, but as kids, we sure thought so. One Christmas, all of us kids stormed out the back door as the adults yelled, "You kids don't go near that pool!" A few minutes later, we were all walking along the edge of the pool. It didn't matter it was covered with a massive sheet of ice and snow; we all stood there and envisioned summer days at Grandma's house. As I looked at the surface, I began to wonder what any normal young boy would: *I wonder if I could walk across this?* Captivated by the thought, I began to test it by pressing as hard as I could with my hands and feet. It seemed solid enough to me. I became more drawn to the idea and decided to place my entire body weight on it while holding on to the edge. It didn't budge. Disregarding both the warning from the adults to "*stay away*" and the warnings from my sister and cousins that I would fall through, I was convinced I could do it. About three steps in, the ice cracked, and I sank to the bottom.

Now, I'm not sure how, at nine years old, I ejected myself out of that pool so quickly, but I did. With zero sympathy, my sister and cousins promptly informed me of all the trouble I was in for. I immediately begged my sister to sneak out a towel for me to dry off. Thankfully, she did. Somehow, I also got them all to agree not to tell anyone. Although my jeans were still plenty wet, I was optimistic no one would notice. Once inside, my plan was to go straight to the bathroom and find a blow dryer to seal the deal. Passing through the kitchen, my grandmother looked me up and down and sternly asked, "Did you get in that pool?" Not missing a beat and continuing my trek to the bathroom, I quickly exclaimed, "No! Why would I get in the pool? It's wintertime, Gram!" Believing I was in the clear, my mom asked my sister the same question. With zero hesitation, she ratted me out. "Yep. We all told him not to, but he didn't listen to us!" she happily disclosed. I remember all of this with such clarity because the story was often retold year after year.

I ignored the "*stay away*" directive. Like the lure of sexual temptation, my flesh persuaded me to ignore the instruction to "*stay away*" and I walked off the edge. Fully convinced I could make it to the other side, I also ignored my sister's and cousins' call to *flee*. Then instead of admitting my mistake and repenting for it, I decided to hide and cover up my disobedience.

Stay away *from her! Don't go near the door of her house!*
Proverbs 5:8, NLT

"STAY AWAY" is the first directive the Bible gives us regarding sexual temptation. Is it that simple? Are we going to obey? Do we believe He who created us wants us to succeed and conquer while on this earth? Staying away from all sexual temptation is obedience to God's Word. Staying away isn't the latest "how to get free" tactic, it's the original biblical commandment!

As a side note, if you're struggling with sexual sin and someone courageously calls it out, don't lie! I think about the audacity I had to lie to my family: "No, I didn't get in the pool," as I walked through the house soaking wet. Today, most men are hiding sexual sin. Unlike the outward evidence of wet clothes, sexual sin hides inside the flesh. The purpose of this book is to draw it out of you. Own up to it, confess it, and be rid of it before the enemy destroys you with it.

When Manny Pacquiao and Floyd Mayweather Jr. announced they would box in early 2015, the match was billed as the fight of the century. Mayweather entered as the five-division undefeated world champion, and Pacquiao was the

TODAY, MOST MEN ARE HIDING SEXUAL SIN.

eight-division world champion. The fight was one of the most anticipated sporting events in history. To put it in perspective, each boxer was expected to earn $100 million for this single event. This projection was not only met, it was shattered. It was reported Manny took home approximately $130 million and Floyd a staggering $230 million. I'm not even a boxing fan, but leading up to the big day, I scanned the latest headlines. After learning Manny was a Christian, I became even more intrigued to see how he was fairing leading up to the match.

The day before the fight, I watched the official weigh-in at the MGM Grand in Las Vegas, Nevada on May 2, 2015. When Manny was announced, an older man in a suit walked up to two bikini-dressed supermodels standing on the stage. He tapped one of them on the shoulder and spoke something in her ear. Then, he walked across the stage and did the same to a second set of models. The women looked completely dumbfounded. They awkwardly walked toward the back of the stage and were eventually out of sight by the time Manny came up. After watching this unfold, I asked myself, *Did I see what I think I saw?* Is it possible Manny Pacquiao was practicing Proverbs 5:8 by *staying away*? Or as the NKJV version states, *"Remove your way far from her"* (Proverbs 5:8).

Would a superstar like Manny Pacquiao really go out of his way to do something like that on a national stage? Next, Floyd Mayweather Jr. was announced. The models immediately reappeared and remained there. What's my point? Well, first I'm totally assuming it was Manny Pacquiao's decision to remove them. I honestly can't think of any other reason! Second, these are the kind of "stay away" decisions we are suppose to make every day.

Men, God designed you to be sexual. He designed you to desire sex. Some of you need to quit beating yourself up by questioning why you're like this and realize instead it's by His design. Because of His design, and because He reserves sex for the marriage bed alone, His Word tells us we must stay away from it in every other form. *Stay away* from environments, people, activities, and venues where you believe you will be tempted. Don't purposely set yourself up to fail by walking into a fire. Instead, purpose to *stay away* from what draws you to the flame.

Identify areas where you've been tempted or had previous sexual failures and *stay away* from them.

A few examples:
- → **Avoid being alone with a female other than your wife.**
- → **If you're unmarried, avoid extended alone time with a female or consider a chaperon when needed.**
- → **Don't travel with females alone.**
- → **Avoid social media and leisure technology if it tempts you in any way.**
- → ***Stay away* from venues, movies, games, music, and people that tempt you.**
- → **Cancel your gym membership.**
- → **Don't get online for pleasure or entertainment.**
- → **If you are constantly bombarded with struggles at work and nothing can be done to change it, pray and begin seeking a new job.**
- → ***Stay away* from anything causing you to stumble.**

Some of you may be thinking, *it would be crazy for me to do these things. It is not even possible for me.* Take a moment and read Matthew 5:27-30. Does Jesus really intend for us to "pluck out our eye" or "cut off our hand" to avoid sinning? Or was he illustrating how vigilant He expects us to be against sexual sin? I personally hope and believe it's the latter. If not, the majority of us would be one-eyed and one-handed men! What do you need to "pluck" or "cut" out of your life in regard to sexual temptation? Whatever it is, do it. It's biblical!

The way to Heaven is ascending; we must be content to travel uphill, though it be hard and tiresome, and contrary to the natural bias of our flesh.

~ Jonathan Edwards

Men, we live in a world where convenience is not the way of a righteous man. This world is never going to cater to your needs as a follower of Jesus Christ. In fact, it is doing everything it can to lead you away from Godliness. The way of the world is flowing downstream, and by default, this is where most are headed. Cutting things out in your life will often be difficult and you may feel like you're all alone and paddling upstream. When I started my business in 2007, a state-of-the-art gym had just opened down the street and was offering a promotional

CONVENIENCE IS NOT THE WAY OF A RIGHTEOUS MAN.

lifetime membership to all local business owners. I'm all about good deals and this was a deal for life! So, I jumped on it. However, when I became convinced the Bible instructs us to *stay away* from temptation versus attempting to resist it, I cringed at the thought of having to give up my gym membership. No matter how good I was, or how much I purposed not to look at women, I was consistently faced with "fire" at the gym. My gym membership was incredibly convenient and useful for me. Not only was it literally down the street from my office, but I had lifetime access there and at all of their locations nationwide! Nevertheless, I began to realize I was walking into a blazing inferno every time I entered the doors. So, I cut it off.

Vigilantly cut off venues, entertainment, technology, TV, people, conveniences, relationships, gym memberships or whatever! Be the man who is paddling upstream alone, not the one cruising downstream with everyone else. Jesus said, *"Enter by the narrow gate; for wide is the gate and broad is the way that leads to destruction, and there are many who go in by it. Because narrow is the gate and difficult is the way which leads to life, and there are few who find it"* (Matthew 7:13-14).

YOU ARE MORE LIKELY TO FALL IN THE DARK

Part of my business involves purchasing vehicles for clients. Think of it like a concierge service that saves you money and eliminates the whole car dealership hassle. Wednesday was the day of the largest auto auction in my area. On Tuesday nights, we led a home group for our church, so it was quite late before I sat down to prepare for the early morning auction. I would begin the routine task of combing through the auction list in search of potential matches. Often, I'd be sourcing for as many as twenty clients at a time. It was tedious and time-consuming work. It became something I didn't look forward to and would often pull up other things online to keep myself awake. I would check out college football scores and schedules, look at the real estate and stock markets, and check the latest news headlines and current events–all innocent stuff. Then it happened. A lustful lure hooked me. I clicked on an image at the bottom of a news article and it pulled me deep into the dark waters of pornography.

...Do not stray into her paths; For she has cast down many wounded, and all who were slain by her were strong men. Her house is the way to hell, descending to the chambers of death.
Proverbs 7:25-27

Wait, I thought I was free from this? I couldn't believe I had fallen. At that point in my life, I'd been walking in purity for some time. I had gone through deliverance at my church, confessed all my past sin to my wife, and was free. After this happened more than once, I decided to go away for a few days on sabbatical to spend some time with God and His Word. First, to repent, and second to seek Him. Although I didn't see all the *S.A.F.E.* directives right away, I did find the first one: *Stay Away.* You fall in the dark. *Stay away* from the dark.

Men, did you know you are more likely to fall in the dark? I made a commitment to the Lord and my wife I would no longer prepare for auction on Tuesday nights. I realized it was a place where I had become vulnerable to attack and was getting blindsided by the enemy. My vulnerability was a result of boredom, fatigue, and darkness. Have you ever considered the enemy watches and studies you? *Where can I most easily knock him off course?*

Beginning the following week, I was in my office two hours early to prepare for auction. I no longer walk near the edge of temptation. The *"stay away"* directive is crucial. It's your best opportunity to avoid failure and go straight to victory.

Now, there are times on this earth where you can end up in a situation or an environment where, suddenly, you're faced with "fire to your chest" or find yourself trying to "walk on hot coals" even though you never purposely intended to do so (Proverbs 6:27-28). Start thinking ahead! If you were heading down a path and spotted a blazing inferno, would you simply run into it? Of course not. In my business, this meant I needed to choose to no longer attend a certain auction. One Monday morning, I received a routine sales call from this auction. The lady thanked me for my business and wanted to inform me of the upcoming sales as well as an exciting new perk they were offering. She excitedly told me the *Hooters Girls* would now be on-site serving wings prior to the auction start time. Wow. I thanked her for calling to warn me.

"Warn you?" she questioned. "Yes. I would've been furious if I had been blindsided by this," I responded. I shared Proverbs 6:27 and told her I would never knowingly walk into a fire. Dumbfounded, she quickly told me to have a nice day and hung up. Ten years later, I haven't stepped foot inside that auction. Sure, it was part of my business and a good source of vehicles, but I don't need it. I know who my Provider is.

If you want God's blessing in your life, start doing what His Word says. It could be not going to an event where you know there will be temptation. Or skipping a guy's night to catch the latest action-packed movie because, if you're honest or have checked the reviews, it likely contains sexual content. Or not going to lunch with a female friend or coworker. If you're married, you should always avoid being alone with another woman. Sacrifice could mean stopping some (or all) social media. It means not reading or watching things with sexual content. Bottom line: If you find yourself in an environment where a lustful fire can ignite in your face,

STAYING AWAY IS ALWAYS EASIER THAN FLEEING.

God is telling you to *stay away*. It is your first and best action of defense. Not putting enough effort here will only lead you to situations where *fleeing* will be required. Please catch this: *Staying away* is always easier than *fleeing*. If you're going to become all God has called you to be, you must start following His Word, not your flesh and not the ways of this world.

By *staying away* from sexual temptation, you are safeguarding yourself against sexual sin. Again, this isn't the latest "get free from porn" tactic, it's the Word of God. Proverbs 5:8 instructs us to *"stay away,"* and Romans 13:14 tells us to *"make no provision for the flesh to fulfill its lusts."*

CHAPTER 16

Flee sexual immorality.
1 Corinthians 6:18

Arriving at the auto auction one Wednesday morning, I immediately hit the men's restroom. Above all the urinals are flyers for you to read as you pee. They're promotional enticements to motivate you to buy cars out of a particular lane. For example, *"Free iPad drawing for every 5th vehicle sold in lane 8!"* As I chose an open urinal, I looked up, and the flyer in front of me was a picture of the Dallas Cowboy cheerleaders advertising a drawing for football tickets. I immediately looked down and thought: *Do I physically flee, or is looking down sufficient here?* Now keep in mind, I had to go. I had two cups of coffee and a bottle of water already that morning. Immediately, I thought of Proverbs 6:27: *"Can a man take fire to his bosom, and his clothes not be burned?"* Still looking down, I imagined that flyer as a fiery blowtorch. Would I stand in front of an actual blowtorch spitting fire and believe, if I simply looked down, it wouldn't burn me? Of course not. I'd instantly *flee.* Still peeing, I did what no man desires to do. I constricted whatever muscle stops the flow of urine and quickly transferred a few urinals down.

Do not be wise in your own eyes; Fear the Lord and depart from evil. It will be health to your flesh, and strength to your bones.
Proverbs 3:7-8

Now, you might be thinking, *Really? Seems a bit extreme. Are you that weak?* The answer would be, yes, I am. The Bible tells me: *"Therefore most gladly I will rather boast in my infirmities, that the power of Christ may rest upon me"* (2 Corinthians 12:9). In my world, it may mean I have to pause peeing and move to a different urinal. I don't care if it felt awkward, silly, or unnecessary. I did it because I

TRUE BELIEF PRODUCES VIGILANT OBEDIENCE.

truly believe the Bible and what it tells me about my weak flesh. True belief produces vigilant obedience. Furthermore, do you suppose God reacts when He sees us take His Word seriously? If so, what do you suppose a reaction from God could mean in your life? As a father, what reaction would you have if you secretly witnessed your son or daughter intentionally go out of their way to obey your instructions?

Fleeing is a mental and physical decision to immediately leave the source your flesh is being drawn toward. This directive is crucial. Why? There is a ticking time bomb, and you can't see the countdown clock. When God tells us to *flee* temptation, I hear him saying: *Run! Run as you've never run before. Get out now! Go!* In the Bible, Joseph demonstrates this for us perfectly! Genesis 39:12 says, "*She caught him by his garment, saying, 'Lie with me.' But he left his garment in her hand and fled and ran outside.*" Now, this is a man we can all learn from. He fled right out of his clothes! Most fall to sexual sin not because of the temptation of it, but by failing to *flee* from it.

Staying away and *fleeing* will always be voluntary and against your flesh. Reread that. The truth is, every time you land in a position of temptation, you're in point-blank range for the enemy to take you out.

Point-blank range denotes the distance a marksman can expect to fire a specific weapon and hit a desired target without adjusting its sights. If a weapon is sighted correctly and ammunition reliable, the same spot should be hit every time at point-blank range.
Wikipedia

LOOK DOWN, FALL DOWN

My dad is one of those guys who can do anything. If faced with something he has never done before, he'll step up and figure it out. A few years ago, I had a motorcycle come in on consignment through my business. Now, I didn't normally take motorcycles, but I had a good relationship with the consigner and agreed to sell it for him. A few weeks later, my dad happened to be driving by and saw the overhead door of my warehouse open. I found him straddled over that motorcycle. "What are you doing with this?" he asked.

"I'm selling it for a good client of mine." I said.

"Man, it makes me want one again." he said. Immediately, I saw an opportunity to bless him. I took some time to pray and think it through, especially about how my mom would react. Feeling peace to move forward (and getting my mom's very hesitant approval), I decided to buy it from the consignor. Father's Day was around the corner, and it was the perfect opportunity to surprise my dad. I'll never forget him laying eyes on it as he walked out the front door where we had it parked. He was shocked! What a blessing to be able to do something like that for a dad who has gone out of his way at least a thousand times to help his son. Thanks Dad.

Now, my dad wasn't allowed to touch that bike until he had taken the full motorcycle training and road safety course, a direct order from his wife, my mother. So, about a month later, he was finally on his way. Visiting with him one evening, he went on and on about his newfound excitement of commuting to work. He told me how he had found some back roads to keep him off the highway, another direct order from my mom. Then he said something that instantly resonated within me: "*Look Down, Fall Down.*"

"What does that mean?" I asked.

"Target fixation." he replied.

"The safety course instructor pounded this in us. Don't look down at the road or you will end up there." he explained.

The rule says to look in the direction you want to go. In the context of riding a motorcycle, it means the bike will go where you are looking. My wife is great proof of this. Until my dad shared this wisdom, I was baffled how she would frequently crash into the curbs when we would ride our bicycles. *Ah, there's a curb, there's a curb...crash!* Sweetheart: Quit looking at the curbs! As my dad continued, I couldn't shake how this principle directly correlated with the act of *fleeing* sexual temptation.

Flee also youthful lusts; but pursue righteousness, faith, love, peace with those who call upon the Lord out of a pure heart.
2 Timothy 2:22

Look at this verse in the context of *Look Down, Fall Down*. If you look toward temptation and fail to *flee*, you will end up crashing right into it. This verse tells us to *flee* lust and pursue God's way. Men, the road of lust is a dead-end crash into sexual sin. Instead, choose the way of the Lord and you will experience a great ride in this life filled with righteousness, faith, love, and peace. I want to quickly reinforce this point to all

THE ROAD OF LUST DEAD-ENDS INTO SEXUAL SIN.

men who believe it's okay "to look, but not touch." Meaning, you believe it's possible and permissible to admire the physical beauty of a woman without any lust or sexual arousal arising in you. These men apparently declare an exemption from Matthew 5:28: *"But I say to you that whoever looks at a woman to lust for her has already committed adultery with her in his heart."*

If you're a man who believes you can look and not touch, you're deceived. Do not be Satan's fool. No man's flesh is fireproof against this. When it comes to sexual sin, your flesh will convince you to walk right off a cliff while deceiving your spirit everything is under control. Flee! He who created us gave us this simple directive. I encourage you to become a fleeing expert. Whether it's mentally fleeing a lustful thought, or physically fleeing a tempting environment, the act of fleeing should become a knee-jerk reaction for followers of Christ. In the next few chapters, you will see how the flesh wages war against our spirit when it comes to sexual temptation.

CHAPTER 17

ESCAPE

My eyes are ever toward the Lord, For He shall pluck my feet out of the net.

Psalm 25:15

Years ago, when my son had just learned to ride his bike without training wheels, we went out for a few laps around the neighborhood. He was on his bike, and I was jogging beside him. He suddenly got ahead of me and was heading downhill toward an intersection. "Son, slow down!" I yelled. In a matter of seconds, I realized he hadn't slowed down but was going faster. Like a madman, I sprinted toward him and seconds before his front tire entered the intersection, I grabbed him. Startled by the sudden jolt, he said, "Dad, why are you grabbing me?"

Because you're my son, and I love you.

What if I told you your heavenly Father attempts to do the same for you right before you touch that spinning saw blade called sexual sin? Do you really believe in the supernatural God you say you do?

My desire is for you to fully catch the biblical revelation of God's supernatural escape. I hope you will seal it into your daily walk and allow it to forever change you. As I've previously mentioned, there are a countless number of teachings, books, and sermons on breaking free from the bondage of sexual sin. I believe the biblical truth of *God's escape* is the missing puzzle piece for freedom from sexual temptation and immorality. It's why all the *get-free-from-porn* tactics eventually fizzle out. It is why Christian men who do everything they've been taught continue to fall into sexual sin. It's how an unmuzzled man suddenly finds himself under Satan's grip once again.

If you didn't *stay away* and you didn't *flee*, God's supernatural intervention can give you an *escape* from falling into sexual sin. Not only is He fully capable of supernaturally intervening on our behalf when we're incapacitated by a sexual lure, He is willing and ready to do so. Malachi 3:6 reminds us, *"For I am the Lord, I do not change."* The same supernatural God who gave Abraham the ram caught in the thicket, who rescued three men out of a fiery furnace, who parted the Red Sea, who caused an earthquake to allow two innocent men to escape a prison, and who constantly intervened throughout the Bible, is the same God we worship and serve today. The supernatural God who created your life is the same God who can supernaturally intercede and save it.

When you fail to *stay away* and fail to *flee*, you fall to whatever sexual temptation lured you in. Let me further shine some light on this third biblical directive. What if God showed up right before you clicked on pornography? Or right before you walked into a venue full of temptation? Or at the beginning of a movie with sexual content? Or right before you engaged in sexual immorality of any kind? What if God manifested himself in front of you and said, *"Son, I came to rescue you. You were about to be slaughtered."*

THE ESCAPE DOOR

It was a Friday night. My fiancé (now my wife) and I decided to rent a movie. She had just gotten a new DVD player for Christmas. At the time, it was a top-of-the-line 5-disc turntable player. (Keep in mind this was the year 2000!) I inserted the DVD and we sank into the couch. The movie opened with the normal credits and then all of a sudden the player stopped, and the turntable cycled around to eject the DVD. I got up, pushed it back in, and it picked up from where it left off. Seconds later, it did it again. *Okay, the disc is probably dirty. I'll pull it out and clean it.* I pulled it out, inspected it, and to my surprise, it looked brand new. I wiped it down anyway and reinserted it. A few seconds later, it stopped again. My wife then made quite a statement: "I don't think we're supposed to watch this."

"Seriously? Why would you say that?" I countered.

"Maybe it's a sign from God and He is telling us not to watch it," she said.

I didn't say it, but in my mind, I immediately discounted her statement. *This girl has lost her mind. Her, of all people, saying it's a sign from God. I mean she just recently gave her life to the Lord. Now she's telling me God is pushing the eject button on this movie?* I got up, put it back in and sank back into the couch. She got up, walked off and said, "I'm not watching it."

As I sat there and tried to think of a loving way to tell her she was insane, I realized the movie was playing just fine.

"It's working now, must be okay!" I yelled.

"Okay, I hope you like it." she responded.

Frustrated and sitting there without her, I thought, *What if it is God?* Her unwillingness to watch the movie, and the slight possibility God was involved was enough for me. We never watched that movie. Interestingly, we used that DVD player for another seventeen years and you know what? It never spit out another DVD. Furthermore, nearly every time I tell this story and mention the actual name of the movie, the response is usually, "Yeah, it probably was God. I wish I wouldn't have watched that movie myself."

Do we truly believe Romans 8:31 when it says God is for us and not against us? Do we believe He intends for us to be victorious? Why do we believe He will intercede in our lives in other areas but not in the area of sexual immorality?

For the eyes of the Lord run to and fro throughout the whole earth, to show Himself strong on behalf of those whose heart is loyal to Him.

2 Chronicles 16:9

*No temptation has overtaken you except such as is common to man; but God is faithful, who will not allow you to be tempted beyond what you are able, but with the temptation will **also make the way of escape**, that you may be able to bear it.*

1 Corinthians 10:13

A Supernatural Disruption

As a Christian, you've probably read the two scriptures above at least once, if not multiple times before. Most Christians completely overlook God's offer in 1 Corinthians 10:13. In fact, many times when I'm sharing this scripture, a seasoned Christian guy will interrupt and say: "*Yeah, yeah, I know that scripture. God will not allow me to be tempted beyond what I can bear.*" Many of these same men then start believing: *I must not be*

Christian enough. I continue to fail and can't see how I'm ever going to withstand not falling in this area. Why can't I bear it if God will not give me more than I can bear? I must not be under God's favor. God must be so disappointed by my actions, He has given up on me.

These passages not only tell us temptation can be conquered, but God will provide an escape. I nearly titled this book *The Escape Door*, so listen up! The Bible is not only

THE BIBLE EQUIPS US TO LIVE VICTORIOUSLY ON THIS EARTH TODAY.

something we read to get the backstory of our faith; it actually equips us to live victoriously on this earth today. Ecclesiastes 9:18 states, *"Wisdom is better than weapons of war."* The Bible is God-breathed wisdom. If we read it and walk away thinking, *Well, it doesn't seem to be working for me,* is it possible we need to go back and re-read it? Let me break this one down.

1 Corinthians 10:13:

1. There is not a single temptation unique to you.
2. God is faithful to act.
3. God will intercede on your behalf when He deems necessary to help you avoid falling into the temptation.
4. You were not designed to withstand temptation alone; you were designed to look for God's *escape.*

Is it possible God has sent you an *escape* and you didn't recognize it? I believe there are millions of men fighting desperately for freedom from pornography and other forms of sexual immorality. Yet, they're on the *Grace Train* every week, month, or year. Is it possible God has been desperately trying to get their attention in those moments before giving into temptation? Read the following verse in the context of a man battling a temptation: *"For we do not wrestle against flesh and blood, but against principalities, against powers, against the rulers of the darkness of this age, against spiritual hosts of wickedness in the heavenly places"* (Ephesians 6:12).

WE GO COMPLETELY AGAINST SCRIPTURE AND GOD'S DESIGN WHEN WE ATTEMPT TO FIGHT A SPIRITUAL BATTLE WITH OUR FLESH.

We go completely against scripture and God's design when we attempt to fight a spiritual battle with our flesh. Many of us believe we can win this way, even though God's Word says otherwise. We think we can resist. We think we can look and not touch. Whether we realize it or not, we're setting ourselves up to fail. When we don't *stay away*, and we don't *flee*, we fall. This world knows how weak our flesh is, it's time for us to realize it, too.

Walk in the Spirit, and you shall not fulfill the lust of the flesh. For the flesh lusts against the Spirit, and the Spirit against the flesh; and these are contrary to one another, so that you do not do the things you wish.
Galatians 5:16-17

Will you do something for me? Before you read the sentences in bold below, close your eyes and think back to the last time you had a sexual failure, specifically the moment just before giving into it. Now, imagine God calling out to you. I believe you would hear Him say something like this:

"Son, I came to get you. I didn't design you to withstand the fire about to consume you. The world fully supplies the enemy with a constant and endless supply of sexual temptations to capture you, manipulate you, deceive you, and destroy you. I am for you and never against you. Please, look for me. I am here my son, take my escape."

Men, I hear the cry of our God when He looks down and sees one of His children being lured by Satan. We serve a God who gave His one and only Son to save you and me. We must no longer believe the lie that we are unworthy of His desire to divert us from walking into a fire! No matter how shameful our position is, He will rescue us from it. If you're a believer struggling with any kind of sexual sin, God has been and could still be sending you an *escape*.

CHAPTER 18

SUPER-NATURAL DISRUP-TION

We must be ready to allow ourselves to be interrupted by God.

- Dietrich Bonhoeffer

"I'm on day 126 of my 365-day-porn-free challenge," he excitedly told me at breakfast one morning. Dustin was a young man I had known for several years. As we chatted about his progress, I began to wonder something. "So, what happens on day

366?" I asked. He laughed and said, "Well, hopefully, this creates a permanent healing that lasts forever."

Men, when we're walking in purity, God can do a work inside of us that cannot be done when we're in sin. However, God has never spoken in His Word of our mortal bodies one day becoming immune to sin, or the flesh suddenly becoming fireproof.

FREEDOM FROM SEXUAL SIN IS NOT SOMETHING WE ACHIEVE ONE DAY; IT IS SOMETHING WE'VE ALREADY RECEIVED IN JESUS CHRIST.

Freedom from sexual sin is not something we achieve one day; it is something we've already received in Jesus Christ. Pause. Okay, many of you probably just thought: *Yeah, yeah, I know the blood of Jesus Christ covers my sin.* If this was you, reread it in the context of God supernaturally intervening on your behalf to give you an *escape* before a temptation pulls you in. That is to say, *through* Jesus Christ, *freedom* is available. The majority of men I've talked to over the years admit they've wondered about this. As in, they thought a supernatural disruption may have occurred to stop them from engaging in sexual sin. They go on to inform me of many specific examples where they thought God was intervening. Instead of believing it was God, most dismissed it as random coincidence. Let me propose a question to those who doubt the supernatural God we Christians say we believe in. If you choose to believe the Bible (specifically 1 Corinthians 10:13 where it says, "*God will provide a way of escape*"), are those events coincidences? Who or what other disrupting force in this fallen world would be aiming to prevent you from engaging in sin? Think about it. As I stated in chapter six, this world is never in favor of your morality. God is constantly trying to save us, especially from this world and the enemy who is always out to destroy us. Quit dismissing the supernatural God you say you believe in and start seeking His supernatural *escape*.

Knowing God is your single greatest privilege as a Christian.
~ Sinclair Ferguson

Supernatural disruption is when God disrupts the environment the enemy is about to trap you in. This usually means you failed to *stay away*, and you failed to *flee*. However, this is not always the case. In today's world, we can be instantly blindsided with sexual temptation. It's vitally important we're walking as vigilant, kingdom-minded soldiers while on this earth. We don't always see them, but God sees the pitfalls around us. This is why His Word is filled with wisdom to avoid them.

All sexual freedom teachings and books I've studied say once you fail to *flee*, you will likely fall. They walk you through the process of asking God's forgiveness and accepting His grace. Most then point you to seek a healing ministry, accountability, and get software protection as solutions. This is where we have missed the supernatural intervention contained in 1 Corinthians 10:13: *"God will make a way of escape."* I believe it's the primary reason why Christians eventually hide their struggle with sexual sin. They've gone through freedom classes, deliverance, addiction counseling, men's seminars, submitted to accountability, installed software protection, and read book after book on how to become free. Yet, they find themselves rising up one day only to fall the next. Yes, they experienced freedom, some for long periods of time. However, many end up right back in sexual sin by casually walking off the edge of the mountain they just climbed.

For those of you who would say you've never experienced God trying to get your attention before you engaged in a sexual sin, have you ever thought to look for Him? Have you ever paused before clicking on porn and called out to God? Something like: *"God, I need help. Where is your escape?"* Many of my escapes have resulted from asking God to intervene and sensing His presence leading me to stand up and flee. *God, lead me to your escape.* In my experience, supernatural disruption occurs more like a "wake-up" alarm. It would be similar to God tapping you on the shoulder and saying, *"Hey, time to go!"*

In my business, I frequently hear clients tell me that once they bought their car, they suddenly began seeing the same car all over the place. The truth is: They never saw it before, because they weren't looking. It wasn't until they purchased their car that

THE MESSAGE PREACHED TODAY FOR AVOIDING SEXUAL IMMORALITY COMPLETELY UNDERVALUES GOD'S WORD AND HIS SUPERNATURAL PROVISION.

they noticed others like it. The same can be said for God's escape doors. It's possible you've never seen one because you're not looking for one. Begin looking for them. Next time you are trapped in sexual temptation, look for and take His *escape*.

The message preached today for avoiding sexual immorality completely undervalues God's Word and His supernatural provision. There's been little mention of the *supernatural* step only God can provide. Telling a man he can be "healed" from sexual temptation is unbiblical. The blood of Jesus covers all our sins and absolutely heals us from our past. However, the Word of God never speaks of a "fireproof flesh" on this side of eternity.

We cannot treat sexual sin the same way we treat other sins or addictions. It's a different animal. Why? Because it's a one-of-a-kind incapacitating sin (1 Corinthians 6:18). Today, counseling is big business and sexual sin has been grouped right in with everything else. This would be like your veterinarian expanding his practice to include humans!

All sarcasm aside, please don't misunderstand me. Some of you need serious intervention. Counseling and deliverance can be life-changing for those with deep wounds, strongholds or generational iniquities. I am in no way against Christian counseling! However, when we attempt to treat sexual sin as just another sin or addiction, we have failed to believe it's a one-of-a-kind sin. God never spoke of our flesh one day becoming resistant from this type of sin. "Healing" and "freedom" from this sin only occurs by constantly obeying His Word and staying in His presence! According to 2 Corinthians 3:17, *"Now the Lord is the Spirit, and where the Spirit of the Lord is, there is freedom"* (NIV). Did you catch it? Freedom occurs where God is.

All Scripture is given by inspiration of God, and is profitable for doctrine, for reproof, for correction, for instruction in righteousness, that the man of God may be complete, thoroughly equipped for every good work.
2 Timothy 3:16-17

If you just blew past the scripture above, go back! It is the foundation of truth this book is built upon. God's perfect instructions are found in His Word. People want answers to their problems, but they don't truly believe the Bible actually has them. If you're honest, you've thought the same thing at some point in your life. We often treat the Bible like a buffet line. We go through and take what we are familiar with or what makes us feel good, but we leave behind what we're unsure of or what we don't like. In his book, *Why Revival Tarries,* Leonard Ravenhill puts it this way: *"One of these days, some simple soul will pick up the book of God, read it, and believe it. Then the rest of us will be embarrassed."* Why? Because all the answers to life are there.

As I've already said a few times now, a countless number of books, teachings, opinions, and strategies have been put forth on how to get free from sexual temptation. Why would God create so many different and ever-changing strategies to get free from one particular sin? Is it possible He wasn't aware how bad it would one day become? Were His original instructions not enough? Is He innovating ways to keep up with the technologies and trends of this day and age? Why are there so many solutions being preached, yet sexual sin continues to burn out of control?

Jesus Christ is the same yesterday, today, and forever.
Hebrews 13:8

His Word has always contained the solution to this battle. 1 Corinthians 10:13 tells us God *"will make a way of escape."* It's right there in the Bible. In Matthew 4:1-4 when Jesus is tempted in the wilderness, He counters Satan with this: *"It is written, 'Man shall not live by bread alone, but by EVERY word that proceeds from the mouth of God."* What we're leaving behind on the buffet line is the very food meant to fuel our spirit. Quit choosing only what satisfies your flesh or is easily digestible and start eating the entire Word of God. Psalm 119:9 says, *"How can a young man cleanse his way? By taking heed according to Your word."* God's Word sustained Jesus when He walked the earth, and God intends for it to do the same for us. This is why Christian men continually fall into sexual sin. They're not applying the original biblical directives God gives us in His Word to overcome it: **Stay Away. Flee. Escape.**

This is your moment to take hold of this truth. God can give you an escape from falling to temptation. He can pull you out supernaturally. God's *escape* has been the missing piece for most of you. Many of you who seek purity and fight sexual temptation with all your power, determination, and grit are baffled at how you still fall so easily. Wake up! It's not only about what *you* can do. You were never designed to win without Him. You minus God equals failure. I'm not talking in the context of truly accepting Christ as your Savior. If you've haven't, then yes, it is required! I'm talking about being aware of His presence in the exact moment you're about to fall to temptation. Our part is natural, His part is supernatural. Overcoming sexual temptation requires supernatural intervention if you haven't *stayed away* or *fled* from it. Did you know most of us already believe God can supernaturally intervene? I'll prove it to you. How do I know? By the way we've all prayed.

> *God, help me resist my desires.*
> *God, give me the strength I need to withstand.*
> *God, remove my desire for sex until I'm married.*
> *God, make my eyes only desire my wife.*

GOD'S ESCAPE HAS BEEN THE MISSING PIECE FOR MOST OF YOU.

God, remove temptation from my path.
God, blind my eyes to anything tempting me.

We will ask God to supernaturally alter us, change our circumstances, and allow our flesh to withstand fire; but we are hesitant to believe He will rescue us when we are being lured into the fire. As 2 Timothy 3:5 suggests, *"do we only say or act like we believe?"* Do we have a form of godliness but don't actually believe enough to engage His supernatural power? If you're ever going to live the supernatural life the Bible speaks of, it's going to involve God's supernatural intervention.

Allow me to insert a warning here. Satan will always come to deceive us regarding the possibility of God supernaturally disrupting your environment. *God interrupting the environment? Come on. Internet connection freezes, you seriously think that's God? Just because your wife called right in the middle of you looking at pornography doesn't mean God caused it. Go ahead, proceed, and get your fix.* If the enemy can convince you to ignore, disregard, or overlook these so-called disruptions, you will fall.

KNOW YOUR POSITION

Have you ever thought: *I'm going to forgo putting gas in my car. I bet there is a chance it will continue to operate without it.* (To all electric car owners: try to remember your old car!) A gas-powered vehicle requires fuel to operate. We wouldn't imagine we could override its design and operate it without gas. In the realm of sexual temptation, you are designed to need Him. Have you been leaving God behind in your pursuit of freedom from sexual sin? He is the only fuel capable of igniting us to *Stay Away*, *Flee*, and *Escape*. Many of you have been stuck for years, wondering why you can't progress in this battle. Like a car with no gas, you'll never reach your destiny without Him.

Today, I anticipate escape doors in my life. If you were to get inside my head when I'm blindsided with a temptation, you'd start to believe I had a wireless connection right into the throne room of God Almighty.

> *Lord, show me a way out.*
> *Lord, open an escape door.*
> *Father, highlight your path.*
> *God, send me the coordinates to get out of here!*

Men, there is victory when you operate the way God designed you to operate. Proverbs 21:31 says, *"The horse is made ready for the day of the battle, but victory rests with the Lord."* Many Christians charge ahead believing they are equipped for battle. They truly believe Philippians 4:13: *"I can do all things through Christ who strengthens me."* However, the fatal mistake made by most is they foolishly leave God behind! They engage in the fight instead of positioning themselves behind Christ, their defender. We were designed to do all things *through* Christ who gives us strength.

The greatness of a man's power is the measure of his surrender.
~ **William Booth**

Know your position! In this fight you must learn to position yourself behind Christ. He designed you to need Him. Sexual temptation is a battle YOU cannot win without HIM. Think of tag-team wrestling. In a moment of temptation, tag in Almighty God, flee the

SHAME WILL CAUSE YOU TO HIDE FROM GOD INSTEAD OF RUNNING TO HIM.

ring, and allow God to obliterate Satan. Remember, sexual sin is a one-of-a-kind sin against your flesh. When you inflict yourself with it, shame will incapacitate you. Shame will cause you to hide from God instead of running to Him.

The next time you find yourself in a moment of temptation, humble yourself and look for an escape. If you have already sinned, call upon Him to intervene anyway! He is that good. Renew your mind and start believing the Bible. God is never against us! He is absolutely willing and ready to come to your rescue. If someone or something disrupts you on the way to sinning, who or what else could it be in a world completely against you? Quit believing those random disruptions are just natural coincidences. There is nothing natural about them–they are supernatural.

On page 241, I've included a guide on how to receive, recognize and respond to God's escape.

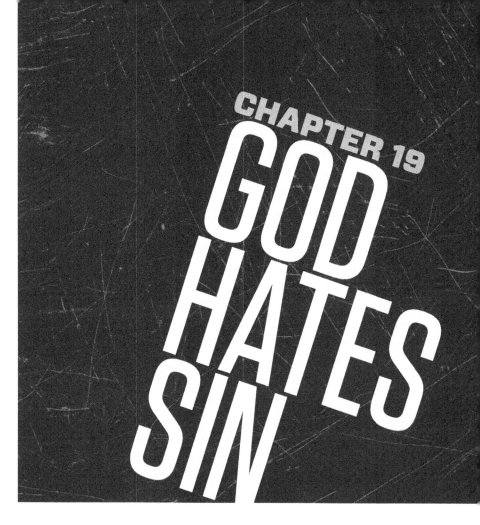

CHAPTER 19
GOD HATES SIN

When I grow up, I'm going to be a doctor.

All through high school and most of college, I worked hard to convince myself it was God's calling on my life to become a doctor. However, if I was honest with myself back then, it had nothing to do with God and everything to do with one day owning an NSX! In the small Texas town where I grew up, the only guys with high-end sports cars were doctors. So, when I got to college, I picked the best sounding pre-med degree on the list: Cell & Molecular Biology with a minor in Chemistry.

Since then, I've offered to give my degree back. It's another story, but on a sabbatical one year, I sensed the Holy Spirit urge me to list out all my unconfessed sin and everyone who I've wronged. Yep, you can imagine where that led. That year I confessed sin, paid recompense, humiliated myself multiple times, and tried to give both my undergraduate and graduate degrees back. Why? I cheated and manipulated my way through several classes. For that one, I was put in touch with the Officer of Academic Integrity at my university. At first, she literally thought it was a prank call. "Sure, a student turning himself in for cheating. Good one, who is this?" she laughed. After finally convincing her I was serious, she admitted she didn't know what to do. "I've never had a student call to report himself," she said. She took my information and assured me she would be in touch. I guess she really didn't know what to do because that was several years ago, and those pieces of paper are still in my attic.

Okay, back to where I was originally going with this. On the first day of my sophomore year, I entered the crowded lecture hall of a Chemistry class and sat in the first open seat I saw, right next to Amber. After class, she turned toward me, introduced herself, and asked if I wanted to be study buddies. I instantly accepted. Amber was attractive, and I needed a study buddy. It started with us meeting at the library on campus. Several weeks later, she invited me to her house for dinner. Amber was nearly twice my age, recently divorced, and was going back to school to further her career. She was a great person and at first, I truly saw her more as a friend. However, the invitation to meet at her house changed something.

Sitting at the dining room table and watching her prepare dinner, I suddenly began desiring to be more than study buddies with Amber. Until that night, all Amber and I had ever talked about were electron structures! That evening, we put Chemistry aside and enjoyed learning more about each other. The next week, I decided to invite her over to my apartment to study.

When I opened the door, I quickly realized I was in trouble by the way she was dressed.

I immediately sat down and attempted to get right into studying. Without sitting down, she took off her shoes, walked over and said, "Is studying really what you had in mind when you invited me over?" I'm sure I said something smooth (probably stupid), but the only thing I remember is the quick and random disclaimer she gave seconds before I moved in to kiss her. "Okay, it's not a big deal, but I do have HSV-1," she sweetly whispered.

Now, I didn't have a clue what HSV-1 was, and at that moment, I didn't care. What I heard was: *I have a disease and there's a chance you will die if you touch me!* My flesh was instantly deactivated. True story! Without even offering her the chance to explain, I quickly escorted her to the door. I told her it was probably best if we discontinued studying together. Sadly, I didn't even try to sugarcoat it. I literally remember thanking her for saving my life! She quickly put her shoes on, called me a random assortment of names, and walked out. I stood at the doorway to make sure she was off safely. It was dark, and I didn't live in the nicest apartment complex. Even though I now saw her as a deadly temptress, for some reason, I still wanted to make sure she was safe.

As I sank into my couch, I couldn't help but believe God reached right into my apartment to save me from making a mistake. In the same breath, I both repented and praised Him. The next day, Amber stopped me after class and bluntly asked if I even knew what HSV-1 was?

"No, not exactly," I admitted.

"It means I get fever blisters on my lips sometimes!" she jeered as she quickly disappeared in the crowded hallway.

I cannot describe what I felt watching her walk away. Part of me wanted to chase her. *That's it? I can handle fever blisters!* But the other part of me knew to stay away. Back then, I didn't have a clue about God's *escape*. Still, I couldn't shake it was simply a coincidence she described "fever blisters" in such a way that made them sound like a deadly disease. Who does that? Today, there is no doubt in my mind that "HSV-1" was an *escape door*. It deactivated my flesh.

There is a direct connection to the appearance of an escape door and the battle between your flesh and spirit. If the flesh overtakes your spirit, you're sunk. Therefore, you must look for and take the *escape* immediately. 2 Corinthians 10:3-4 *says, "For though we walk in the flesh, we do not war according to the flesh. For the weapons of our warfare are not carnal but mighty in God for pulling down strongholds."* Right there, in the Bible, a revelation is given to us for this battle.

AN ESCAPE ENCOUNTER WITH GOD FREES YOU IN A MOMENT, BUT MORE SIGNIFICANTLY REVEALS HIS SUPERNATURAL PRESENCE IN YOUR LIFE.

Satan knows when we tap into God, God will grab us out of sexual temptation. Jesus tells us in John 6:63, *"It is the Spirit who gives life!"* This is the escape door revelation. Once you experience God's supernatural disruption in this area of your life, a mind-shift can occur inside you regarding sexual sin. It's this mind-shift that can transform you. Experiencing an escape will bring Romans 8:31 to life: *"What then shall we say to these things? If God is for us, who can be against us?"* Please catch this. God is so seriously against the destructive powers of this sin, He will disrupt heaven and earth to stop it. Experiencing this will change your mind about sexual sin. An *escape* encounter with God frees you in a moment, but more significantly reveals His supernatural presence in your life. Furthermore, if you've ever doubted God exists, this will certainly ignite your belief. Your belief in God will go to an entirely new level. I know mine did. Over twenty years later, I still remember walking back into my apartment that evening thinking, *"There really must be a God."*

Allow yourself to start believing He desperately loves you, even amidst sexual immorality. This will transform how you view God and sexual sin. God hates sin because it separates us from Him. The Holy Spirit inside you desperately desires for you to hate sin. Hating sin is the key that unlocks what every Christian man who genuinely begins to pursue God eventually prays for: *God, help me not to sin. God, make my desires pure. God, change me!* Once you begin to hate sin as God hates sin, you will transform from a flesh-pleasing man to a God-pleasing man. Read that sentence again!

IF YOU'RE BATTLING TEMPTATION AND HAVE NOT YET FALLEN, FLEEING IS STILL ON THE TABLE!

If you decide to believe and carry out the biblical instructions outlined in this book, let me warn you: There is no guarantee of an *escape* if you didn't *flee*. Some of you have already tried this. *Well, I'm going to click on this link, watch this movie, go to this venue, or fantasize on these thoughts until something happens. God, if you don't somehow get my attention soon, I guess I'm not worth saving.* First, let me propose a question. In the moment just before you are to engage in sexual sin, is it possible you still can *flee*? If you're battling temptation and have not yet fallen, *fleeing* is still on the table! Don't think for another second this book is the next latest and greatest *how-to-get-free-from-porn strategy* or some unlimited pass to fleece God to bail you out. If you do, you will miss the entire revelation here. Go back and reread 1 Corinthians 10:13. It indicates God provides an escape when you are tempted beyond what you are able to bear. If no escape door appears, then you are still able to bear and flee from it.

Before we move on, allow me to reiterate the first directive: *Stay Away.* This is your number one doorway to sexual purity every time. The only way you will ever become vigilant about staying away, is to hate sin the way God hates sin. When I invited Amber over, I was fully aware I was setting myself up to fall. Picture Satan attempting to push you off a cliff. If you are not near the edge, and you

HATING SIN AS GOD HATES SIN IS THE ROAD TO FREEDOM FROM SIN.

purpose to *stay away* from the edge, his chances are diminished. Sure, he could taunt you, but he can't physically push you. He is only capable of enticing you off the edge. He has no real power over you, it's all a facade. If you're standing at the edge of temptation, his task becomes much easier to cause you to slip.

The Bible tells us Satan tempted Jesus when He was near an edge. This happened on the pinnacle of the temple when he dared Him to jump and again on a high mountain overlooking all the kingdoms of the world (Matthew 4:5-6, 8). However, Jesus responded, *"Away with you, Satan! You shall worship the Lord your God, and Him only you shall serve. Then the devil left Him, and behold, angels came and ministered to Him"* (Matthew 4:10-11). *Stay away* from the edge! If you find yourself near an edge, immediately *flee.* If temptation fills your eyes and begins to flood your *fleeing power* (your physical ability to flee), look for or cry out to God for an *escape*. Satan will leave, and angels will enter.

Allow me to express this once again. When you see God intervene and save you, it will ignite a fire in you to hate sin. This is the fear of the Lord (Proverbs 14:27). It can supernaturally turn your desire to sin into the desire to obey. Hating sin as God hates sin is the road to freedom from sin.

PART 3
DO YOU REALLY BELIEVE?

LIFE INSUR-ANCE

CHAPTER 20

*Trust in the Lord with all your heart and
lean not on your own understanding;
In all your ways acknowledge Him,
and He shall direct your paths.*

Proverbs 3:5-6

In the original Hebrew text, "trust" and "acknowledge" in the scripture above is translated as "rely on" and "recognize" Him. The escape door is just that. Picture a man who is about to be shot with the fiery dart of sexual temptation. He is about to click on pornography or engage in something he knows he shouldn't. Time is fleeting, and he is seconds away from giving in. Do you believe God could be at work attempting to disrupt his trajectory? His phone rings. It's his dad, with whom he's been hoping to be reconciled with. The power flickers and shuts down the internet connection. A text from a fellow brother with an encouraging scripture comes right before he is about to enter a tempting environment.

You see, I have had many escape door experiences, more than I have relied on or recognized I'm sure. As you read this book you're being presented with the biblical revelation of His *escape*. For me, it was born out of a persistent desire to truly break free from all sexual temptation and sin in my life. One of my earliest escape door experiences was when the DVD player kept spitting out that movie my fiancé and I rented. Over twenty years later, I am still convinced it was the Lord was giving us a way out. That DVD player is now buried in our garage because I can't bring myself to let it go. Many times, I've failed to *stay away* and failed to *flee*. I've clicked on links or images only for the computer to suddenly freeze up. This happened enough times that I began wondering, *could God be intervening?* Other times, I clicked on a link sure to be full of sexual images only to be directed to a completely different

HIS ESCAPE NOT ONLY SAVES YOU FROM A MOMENT OF SEXUAL IMMORALITY, IT AWAKENS YOU TO HOW SERIOUSLY GOD IS AGAINST IT.

webpage. I remember thinking: *Could God be trying to give me a way out?*

The moment I believed it was God disrupting heaven and earth to open an escape door for me, was the moment I caught the *fear of the Lord* (Proverbs 14:27). Please catch this: His *escape* not only saves you from a moment of sexual immorality, it awakens you to how seriously God is against it. Once you wholeheartedly believe God is for you and fiercely against sin, you will never want to fall again. His intervention will ignite you toward becoming the righteous and pure man you are called to be. People often ask me, "*Why do you take this so seriously?*" It's simple. I genuinely *believe* now. My eyes have been opened, and I see how deadly sexual sin is. I cannot help but be vigilantly and aggressively against it now. God is truly real to me now. When you live out what you say you believe, He is faithful to reveal Himself to you.

Will you put this book down for a moment and pray this prayer: *God, I invite you to be the authority in my life, especially in this area. I ask for you to forgive me of all my sins. I ask for your path to freedom from all sexual immorality. Reveal the escape doors you've given me in the past and help me recognize them in the future. God, seal your directives of staying away, fleeing, and your escape in my walk with you. May it be permanently imprinted on my soul. Spiritually reset my thinking toward You and Your ways. Father, I give you full authority to supernaturally disrupt my life from this day forward.*

Today, the church is flooded with *wet matches* who have little belief God is actually going to show up in their lives. They sign up for or continue in Christianity as more of a life insurance policy than a personal relationship with God. To these guys, going to church and professing Christianity keeps their policy active.

Men, God's *escape* only becomes visible to those genuinely and diligently desiring true intimacy with Him. When I became convinced God was intervening and giving me escape doors, I began to see many of them throughout my past. However, I could only see them in the latter years of my struggle. As I thought back to my teenage and young adult years of struggling with pornography, I couldn't recall a time where God disrupted the environment to save me. Psalm 91:14 says, *"Because he loves me,"* says the Lord, *"I will rescue him; I will protect him, for he acknowledges my name"* (NIV). Honestly, in those early years, I didn't believe enough to look for an *escape*, and I certainly didn't call upon God to supernaturally intervene on my behalf in this area. Ecclesiastes 7:26 says, *"He who pleases God shall escape from her, but the sinner shall be trapped by her."* Don't get me wrong, I called myself a "Christian" in those days, but I was a wet match. I was hiding from Him and ignoring His commandments. Just like the first man who walked the earth hid from God, my shame led me to hide, too. The thought of God attempting to rescue me from sexual immorality wasn't even on my radar. I cringe wondering about the escape doors I've missed in my life—those times when I was purposely away from God instead of diligently seeking Him. Until you quit hiding from God, how will you ever see if He is sending you a way out?

The closer you get to God, the more conscious you are to your sin. The glory of His presence shines in dark areas.

- Dr. Ted Roberts

Like many young men today, I believed sexual immorality was normal and God's "grace" allowed for it. I also believed once married, I would be free of it. This is the deception of Satan. It's equivalent to believing a minor who has become an alcoholic will suddenly become sober once he is of legal age. When God created sex, it was, and still is, reserved for one man and one woman who are in a covenant marriage. Outside of that, it wraps explosives around you whether you realize it or not. They may not explode right away, and most times you won't even know they're there.

However, believe the Bible when it says sexual sin is unlike any other sin: It's against your own body. One day, these explosives ignite and your sins will be exposed (Numbers 32:23). Sexual sin always yields pain with lasting scars.

REWARDS

A few years ago, we were planning to take our kids on a surprise trip. They had been working hard to earn this trip as a reward for perfecting their table manners. They didn't know Mommy and Daddy had booked the trip a month prior because of a great discount offer we got through an email. Instead of telling them the day we booked it, we told them if they worked hard on their table manners for the next four weeks, we would take them on a surprise trip. Brilliant, right? Did you

GOD HAS ALREADY BOOKED TRIPS, ACTIVITIES, PROMOTIONS, PROVISION, AND BLESSINGS FOR YOU.

know God has already booked trips, activities, promotions, provision, and blessings for you?

I wonder how many opportunities or blessings I may have missed out on? As a father, it would have broken my heart if my children had missed the mark and we had to cancel their trip. Now, I'm not talking about the "good" that can happen to anyone whether they're following Christ or not. God said in Matthew 5:45 that the sun would rise on the good and the evil, and rain would fall on the just and the unjust. I'm talking about God's blessings, not worldly freebies. I wonder how many times we have broken the heart of the Father? Can I encourage you, or better yet, awaken you to quit treating Christianity as some life insurance policy! God desires to be involved in your life! Many have professed Christianity just in case the Bible is actually real. Today, too many "Christians" live this way. Recently, I asked a guy who was doing some work for me if he was a believer. "Yes sir, I'm a Christian." he responded. After about twenty minutes, I learned he attended church when he could, but definitely on Easter and Christmas. He was sexually active with his girlfriend and was addicted to pornography and video games. Men, until you surrender and obey God's entire Word and all He calls you to do, you will remain a muzzled man holding a wet match. Let me put it another way: A passive and powerless dud for the kingdom of heaven. I don't know about you, but when I get to heaven, I don't want to find out what God says when he doesn't say, *"Well done, good and faithful servant."*

There's true believers and then there's make-believers.
~ **J. Vernon McGee**

Today, I'm constantly asking God if any area of my life is out of alignment with His Word. Why? Because my belief in God is no longer some "just-in-case" life insurance policy. I believe now. I'm sold out! I'm a son of God and believe Jesus Christ was nailed to a cross so I could be forgiven and live.

I encourage you to ask yourself:

Do I really believe in God?
Do I believe the entire Bible?
Do I believe in the supernatural ability of God today?
Am I willing to die to follow Christ?

Scripture says we should work out our salvation with fear and trembling (Philippians 2:12). Becoming a Christian is a supernatural change, not a verbal prayer you once recited. The change involves a supernatural and permanent indwelling of the Holy Spirit! There are many who claim to be Christians, but if they're honest, it's just in case the whole Heaven and Hell thing is real when they die. Many in this group get all dressed up once or twice a year, load up the family and head to church! Others adopt some aspect of Christianity that makes them feel good, and then somehow use God's grace to "white-out" scripture they don't agree with. There are also those who believe and know the Word of God, but instead of entering through the *"narrow gate,"* decide to permanently misuse grace to justify their sin and lifestyle choices (Matthew 7:13-14).

Only he who believes is obedient and only he who is obedient believes.
~ **Dietrich Bonhoeffer**

Several years ago, there was a couple in our home group who seemed to be true Christians. They sang in the church choir and purposed to build relationships within the group. After a few years, they quit attending our group due to the busyness of life. We would still run into them at church occasionally, and I would sometimes talk business over the phone with the husband. One day, he called me to get some advice on transporting his vehicle to California. He said there were some promising opportunities there for him. When I asked what his wife thought about moving, he replied, "I didn't tell you? We got a divorce a while back." He went on to admit he was caught cheating and she left him. He told me he had multiple affairs throughout his marriage before he finally got caught. A man I once thought to be steadily pursuing the Lord, was now telling me his divorce was simply a minor hiccup in his life. "I know God has forgiven me and I'm excited to see what He has in store for me in Cali!" he said enthusiastically.

Talk about a desensitization. Now, because his marriage ended, he was free to pursue his dream of moving to California. He truly saw this as a "God thing." This man was truly deceived and ignorant regarding the devastation and consequences of his sexual sin.

Imagine if there was an app you could download that alerted you every time a divorce was filed? According to a study put out by the Pew Research Center, in just the United States alone, you'd be getting an alert about every thirteen seconds! I wonder if this would cause Christians to take God's gift of a covenant marriage more seriously? Would husbands and wives become more proactive to grow and protect their marriage? Would it cause more "Christians" to start believing the bible, especially John 10:10 where it says the enemy is only out to steal, kill, and destroy?

Men, your marriage is under attack. Many of you need to throw away the "I'm a Christian" name tag you put on once a week, and instead permanently put on the headship mantle you were created to bear. Not only do your wives and children desperately depend on this, but it's also the primary witness the world will see for the Kingdom of God. If you truly desire God's best for you, become a Christ-follower, not a policy-holder.

CHAPTER 21
HANG THEM UP

My oldest daughter was five years old when she stopped me one morning as I was walking out the door to work. "Daddy, Daddy. I made this for your office!" she shouted as she handed me a picture she had drawn. My heart melted as I held her in my arms and told her how much I loved her and my new picture. A few days later, she caught me again before heading out and handed me another drawing. For weeks, she continued to supply me with new drawings as I would leave the house. Each time, she would say, "It's for your office."

One Saturday morning, she and I were planning the itinerary for our daddy-date. She immediately told me our first stop should be my office. This didn't surprise me. My son and I had been making frequent stops there during our man-times together. He would often give his sisters a play-by-play of all his adventures as soon as we got home. Once we took an air compressor hose, tied it to a furniture dolly, and created the *Warehouse Racer!* Another time, we took a car from the warehouse to a nearby stadium parking lot where he quite possibly became the first six-year-old to take the steering wheel of a Porsche GT3! Another time we climbed on top of the warehouse roof and skipped around like the chimney sweeps in *Mary Poppins*. So, when my daughter insisted on making a stop at my office, of course I agreed. As we pulled up to the warehouse door, she said, "No Daddy, I want to go to the office, not the warehouse." Although I was surprised, I didn't argue. I needed to slip into the office anyway to check on a pending deal. As soon as I unlocked the door, she quickly went in and began looking around. "Daddy, where are all the pictures I gave you?" she asked.

"Oh, right over here sweetheart," I confidently said as I grabbed them off the bookshelf.

"Daddy, you were supposed to hang them up. I wanted everyone to see them," she said with disappointment in her voice.

I had failed her. Of course I was supposed to hang them up! Why would I simply stack them on a shelf? What was I thinking? That day we began hanging them up. As I admired all her work, I realized it was both a lack of belief and a lack of understanding that caused me to simply stack them on the shelf. I didn't believe it mattered to her what I did, as long as I took them. I certainly didn't believe she was going to one day conduct a surprise inspection for them! Furthermore, I didn't understand her true purpose. She wasn't only after my praise; she wanted me to show and tell everyone who came to my office.

In the same sense, I believe God wants us to display Him in our lives. His Word, His promises, and all He has done for us. Yet many do the same thing I did and stack Him on a shelf. When people enter our lives, they should see Him. It isn't just our praise He is after; He wants others around us to see His presence in our lives.

In the area of sexual immorality, I believe this is the primary reason Christian men don't look any different than non-Christian men. God has given us clear biblical directives to avoid this grip of Satan. However, many of the men I meet with and counsel admit they have read these scriptures but have simply stacked them on the shelf in their mind. They go on to admit they've had a lack of belief and understanding regarding God's Word in this area of sin, especially the supernatural *escape*.

"Though you grind a fool in a mortar with a pestle along with crushed grain, Yet his foolishness will not depart from him."
Proverbs 27:22

SEXUAL SIN MAY SATISFY A TEMPORARY LUST IN YOUR FLESH, BUT IT FUELS AN EXPLOSIVE DISASTER IN YOUR LIFE.

According to this verse there are men who will read and even believe the message, the warning, and the reproof in this book, yet foolishly stack it on a shelf. Christian men who fall into this category will remain muzzled fools outside of God's covering and calling. Unfortunately, these men usually suffer painful consequences during their lifetime on this earth. Sexual sin may satisfy a temporary lust in your flesh, but it fuels an explosive disaster in your life. Some likely examples include divorce, wayward children, physical and mental health issues, public humiliation, or even jail time (like my NSX friend). Muzzled men are all on the same road: A downhill and dead-end road to destruction. God's Word tells us in 2 Peter 2:21 that men such as this would have been better off not knowing the way of righteousness than to know and backslide into sin.

Quit shelving the biblical sword God has given you. It's meant to be used and seen in your life! Specifically, with respect to the *escape*, I've written many of them down. Hang them up and start soaking in His presence. I've come to realize it's not just for us to see, it's also for others. Imagine if you had something plastered on your wall about how God intervened in your life. Do you think it could ignite a conversation with someone who saw it?

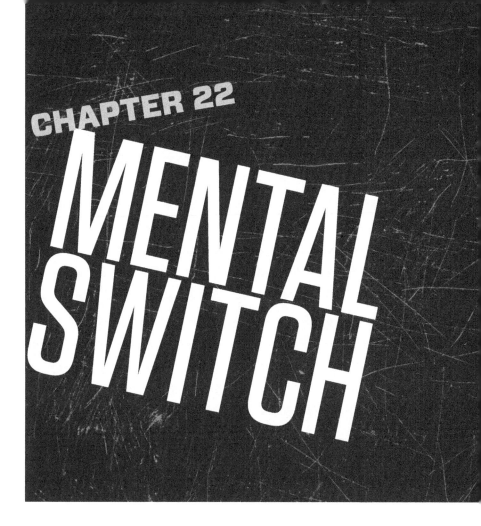

CHAPTER 22
MENTAL SWITCH

What if God gave you an ON/OFF switch for the flesh?

I'll never forget the excitement, anticipation, and the unknown outlook on life I felt standing beside my wife moments before our first child was born. Suddenly, the nurse said, "I see him. He's got a head full of hair!" At that moment, everything in my world immediately stopped. I'll never forget it. I could feel myself crossing a supernatural threshold: *Fatherhood*. When the nurse spoke those words, it was because she physically saw my son in the birth canal. There had been sonograms, but until this day, no one had physically seen him with their own eyes. This was his first appearance on the earth. I'll never forget the overwhelming amazement I felt standing there. Tears began streaming and I was overcome with gratitude toward God for blessing us with a child. Our doctor arrived and took his position. With one final push, my son would be born, and I would be responsible for this child.

Behold, children are a heritage from the Lord, The fruit of the womb is a reward. Like arrows in the hand of a warrior, So are the children of one's youth. Happy is the man who has his quiver full of them; They shall not be ashamed, But shall speak with their enemies in the gate.
Psalm 127: 3-5

Seconds away from my son's birth, I envisioned an ON/OFF switch right in the middle of my chest. I sensed the Holy Spirit: *"If you keep this switch turned off, you will be the husband and father I called you to be."* In other words, become *selfless*.

We all have this *self-switch* inside us. If turned ON, we focus on ourselves and our fleshly desires. Turned OFF, we are led by the Holy Spirit within us, and focus on others. That day, I believe the Holy Spirit was reminding me to be selfless in my role as a husband and father. Yes, I've flicked it ON more times than I'd like to admit, however I've learned to quickly switch it OFF. Now five children later, I can't even find the time to turn it ON!

GOD DESIGNED SEX FOR MARRIAGE ALONE.

In addition to the self-switch, I have found another switch: My *sex-switch*. Do you believe sex is solely reserved for a covenant marriage between one man and one woman? The enemy, the world, and many times our own flesh would like to convince us otherwise. God designed sex for marriage alone. So, why are we tempted to look for sex outside of marriage? Does this mean we are not pure, or something is wrong with us? Does it mean we married the wrong woman? If God created sex for our marriage bed alone, why didn't He design us to default to OFF outside of marriage? That would have solved everything, right?

This makes me think of eggnog. I know, another silly analogy, but bear with me for a bit! The only time I drink it is the few weeks leading up to Christmas. Even though I really, really like it, I never buy it any other time. It's as if the Christmas spirit awakens something inside of me and says, *"It's now time for the eggnog!"* I can honestly say as much as I love it, I've never wrestled with having it outside of this once-a-year occasion. Why is that? It's a twofold answer and it goes far beyond eggnog; in case you're having a hard time relating.

First, I've developed a mental switch that eggnog is for Christmas only. Second, it's been sustainable because I'm never bombarded with it. In fact, I've never seen a display or an advertisement for eggnog except during Thanksgiving and Christmas. As I began writing this, I wasn't even sure you could buy it unless it was during these holidays. I decided to go check. Yep, it's still there. I found one brand in a small quantity. I had to physically hunt for it and overlooked it the first time around. What's my point? If there was a sudden push to start selling eggnog year-round, I'd be in trouble.

Today, I don't have to constantly turn off my "eggnog switch" when I go to the grocery store. I turned it off last Christmas and haven't thought about it since. Furthermore, there hasn't been any outside influence trying to reach inside me to flip it back on. However, if a campaign arose to start promoting eggnog and it was on display all year, it would be a different story. Heaven help me if Costco stocked their supersize jug of it year-round! If I were going to continue my once-a-year eggnog drinking, I would have to mentally flip off my eggnog switch every time I entered a grocery store. I would need to decide up front, "it's not an option." If I unsuspectingly pass by as they're giving away free samples, I would have to *flee!* If it got to the point I couldn't resist purchasing it, I might have to *stay away* from the store all together!

Have you caught my point? Jesus tells us in Matthew 5:28, *"But I say to you that whoever looks at a woman to lust for her has already committed adultery with her in his heart."* I admit it. If eggnog enters my sight at the grocery store, I begin desiring it! If I don't give in, I drive off regretting it!

What's my point? The onslaught of sexual temptation cast before us in this world has become detrimental to men who purpose to walk in sexual purity. Unlike eggnog, sexual temptation is thrust toward us daily. Don't fool yourself. This world is bursting with sexual temptations. My childhood pastor, Jimmy Evans, once gave an appropriate response to the lures, lies, and temptations of the enemy: "Get behind me Satan! I'm not buying what you're selling."

THE ONSLAUGHT OF SEXUAL TEMPTATION CAST BEFORE US IN THIS WORLD HAS BECOME DETRIMENTAL TO MEN WHO PURPOSE TO WALK IN SEXUAL PURITY.

*He who finds a wife finds a good thing, and obtains favor
from the Lord.*
Proverbs 18:22

Sex is reserved for the marriage bed alone. It is the only venue where God grants the privilege and blessing of sex. Outside of marriage, sex is against God's will. Take a moment and read Proverbs 5. Go ahead, it will only take a minute or two.

There is no other sin to which God has given us an ON/OFF switch. Have you ever thought about this? Sex *is a sin* outside a covenant marriage. Sex *is not a sin* inside a covenant marriage. Can you think of any other activity God says is a sin depending on the venue in which it's performed? Proverbs 18:22 tells us marriage has a *"treasure inside."* God tells us this treasure is good and comes with His favor. Ecclesiastes 9:9 tells us *"to live joyfully with our wife."* Genesis 2:25 reminds us *"when we are free of sin, we can stand in pure unashamed nakedness with our spouse."* Proverbs 5 highly encourages us to go all out and enjoy the physical features of our wives! Please catch this. God created sex as a blessing. It's the enemy, the world, and your own flesh flipping it as a sin.

Identify your ON/OFF switch for sex. Thoughts about sex, fantasies about sex, the desire for sex, and actual sex are all fully permissible inside your marriage covenant. Outside of it, it's a sin and your sex switch should be OFF. Stay away from it, flee it and look for God's escape from it. Otherwise, you're flipping your switch ON in a venue God forbids. It's usually at the edge of a cliff with Satan there enticing you to jump. *Stay away* from these edges.

If you're a single man, God's Word informs you this switch is off limits until you're married. Turning it on will yield destruction in your life. Like the serpent tempting Eve to partake of the forbidden fruit, the same serpent is tempting you to flip on this switch. Furthermore, if you're unmarried, did you know you don't even have the right to operate this switch? If sex was created only to exist in a covenant marriage, then engaging in anything sexual as an unmarried man is in direct violation of God's Word. Listen up. This isn't some old-fashioned, outdated, old testament way of life. This is God's way of life. Why do we, as believers, ignorantly believe breaking God's commandments is permissible without consequence? Too many Christians today believe they can smear the blood of Jesus over their willful and reckless habitual sins. I know you would think twice about speeding if you knew there was a police officer positioned up ahead to catch you. Where in the Bible does it say the blood of Jesus exempts you from obeying God's Word?

If you're not married, you are poisoning your future marriage bed when you engage in anything sexual. When you poison His blessings, you ignorantly trade them for curses. Let that soak in a bit. What kind of man would knowingly sabotage his future marriage bed? Don't be fooled by Satan any longer. Don't allow the world to convince you that *"the God who doesn't change"* has lessened or modernized his ways to accommodate today's culture that downplays sexual immorality (Malachi 3:6). If you're single, sex must remain sealed as if under lock and key. Better yet, go buy an actual lock-box, write up a declaration to remain pure for your future bride, and put it inside the box. Then, as an act of obedience and faith, go throw the key off a cliff or something. Keep the box somewhere you will see it every day. Pick it up every day as you pray for your purity. Allow it to remind you of your commitment to both God and your bride-to-be. If you persevere, what a blast it will be busting it open with your bride one day. Of course, this may seem like a ridiculous thing to actually do. But, I believe God loves to respond when He sees you ridiculously obey His Word. Furthermore, I can't imagine there's a woman on the planet that wouldn't hold you in high honor the moment she holds your declaration in her hands. In fact, if you're a man who decides to carry this out, I will stand with you. If you will email your name, phone number and a picture of your declaration statement and lock-box to purity@unmuzzledmen.com, I will personally pray for you. If you are a father, I encourage you to do something like this with your children. Whether it's a purity ring or a lock-box, boldly take a stand for their purity as the pastor of the home. Why wouldn't you?

ALLOWING SEXUAL THOUGHTS, TEMPTATIONS, AND LUST INTO YOUR LIFE OUTSIDE YOUR MARRIAGE BED WILL ALWAYS YIELD DESTRUCTION.

Remember the table saw from chapter fourteen? How foolish I'd be to think I could feather my finger across the top of a spinning table saw blade. Allowing sexual thoughts, temptations, and lust into your life outside your marriage bed will always yield destruction. It may not manifest itself as sin with one thought or one glance, but it poisons your mind with the intent to produce damage. Why would you walk toward a table saw with the intent to touch the blade? Like that piece of wood being pulled and guided by a saw blade, so are we when we entertain temptation. *Stay away* from all things sexual when you're in OFF mode. The Bible states, *"Do not stray into her paths"* for you will *"die for lack of instruction"* (Proverbs 7:25, 5:23).

FLESH AND SPIRIT DEPOSITS

Picture your sexual being as a balance scale inside you. On one side is your spirit, and on the other is your flesh. Every time you decide to turn your sex switch off, to pray against attacks from the enemy, and to take a stand against sexual thoughts and temptations, deposits are made to your spirit. On the other hand, every time you allow a thought to linger, look at a woman lustfully, look at pornography, or allow sexual temptation of any kind in your life, deposits are made to your flesh. At the end of a day or a week, what does your scale look like? If you constantly kept your sex switch off outside your marriage bed, your spirit is overflowing, and you feel like the conqueror the Lord created you to be. If you didn't, your flesh is bursting, and you feel like a caged wild animal. This is when you

A QUICK GLANCE OR THOUGHT ONE DAY CAN TRIP YOU TO FALL ON YOUR FACE IN SEXUAL SIN THE NEXT.

can't seem to get rid of lustful thoughts or resist temptation. It's when the "need" for sex consumes you. Eventually, the flesh overtakes your spirit, and you fall. Never forget sexual sin is a one-of-a-kind sin. It incapacitates you. Men, the reason you get caught in cycles where you can't resist masturbating or having sex, is because you've allowed lustful deposits into your flesh. It doesn't take much either. A quick glance or thought one day can trip you to fall on your face in sexual sin the next. Matthew 26:41 tells us to *"watch and pray, lest you enter into temptation. The spirit indeed is willing, but the flesh is weak!"*

When you make the decision not to look at a woman jogging by, the moment passes almost immediately. However, if you take even the quickest glance, your thoughts continue beyond the millisecond in which you barely looked. The flesh keeps your mind on her. You probably didn't even look long enough to recognize anything about her beyond her shape. However, your flesh convinces you it was a highly attractive woman. Before you know it, you're fantasizing and making lustful deposits about her into your flesh.

I have made a covenant with my eyes; Why then should I look upon a young woman? For what is the allotment of God from above, and the inheritance of the Almighty from on high? Is it not destruction for the wicked, and disaster for the workers of iniquity? Does He not see my ways, and count all my steps?
Job 31:1-4

This passage reminds me of when I would foolishly pray for God to supernaturally modify my eyes. *Change me Lord! Allow me to only see my wife*. The truth is, God has given us the choice to make this covenant so one day we become men who walk in the full armor and obedience to which He has called us. If He simply turned off or manipulated our flesh, it would take away the whole purpose of true obedience and our genuine pursuit of God. God didn't mis-create us. He doesn't need to redesign our flesh for us to become righteous. Instead, God gives us the choice to follow Him in this fallen world. Let that soak in. Men, we must recognize our mental switch for sex and begin choosing to keep it off when we're outside our covenant marriage bed. We live in a time where the enemy is rapidly gaining ground. He has taken our God-given design and desire for sex and is destroying us with it. Make the decision to keep your switch off every single minute you're outside the marriage bed.

What does it look like to turn off your switch? It takes building it into your daily routine and declaring God's truth over yourself every single day. Initially, it may be a mental decision to reach inside you and turn it off. Envision yourself doing it. I include this in my daily morning prayer. Every single day before I leave my house to enter the world, I pray. Just like my car will not back out of the driveway unless I put it in reverse, I've convinced myself I can't leave the same driveway unless I've surrendered myself, my wife, my children, my home, my business, and my entire day to God in prayer. I ask God to go before me, protect me, and lead me. Sometimes it takes two minutes and other times it takes ten minutes. During this time, I ask God to intervene in my life. I mentally turn off my sex switch. I pray: *God, have your way in my family and me. I yield all to you. I give you full permission and authority to interrupt my day in any way. Help me to recognize your escape doors today if needed.* This may seem simple or unnecessary to some of you, but when sexual temptation crosses my path, I'm almost immediately taken back to sitting in my driveway and deciding to turn off my sex switch. Talk about fueling my spirit to cause me to *stay away* and *flee!* Eventually, this switch moves from your flesh side to your spirit side. I went from constantly needing to turn it off, to it defaulting to OFF! Why? Because obedience to God's Word and His directives work. When you pursue righteousness and make deposits in your spirit, the spirit overtakes the flesh and puts it in its place.

A SEXUAL BOMBARDMENT WORLD

Sexual temptations are no longer just available to us, they are *aimed* at us. Earlier, when I was describing how I'm able to avoid buying eggnog throughout the year, I said it was because I had developed a mental switch for it, and I wasn't constantly bombarded by it. My eggnog switch is easy to leave off year-round. Let me put it this way: I'm not making a mental decision to shut off the eggnog switch before I leave the house every day! Did you know there was once a time in our society when the availability of sexual material was similar? It was available, but you had to go find it. Like eggnog in the off-season, you could still get it, but it wasn't advertised, showcased, or stocked everywhere.

Men, we must be vigilantly against all sexual temptation in our lives today. Every time you see or sense temptation ahead, reach down, and guard your switch. If you become tempted, your switch has been turned on. Flee! Immediately leave the environment you're in. Sex shouldn't be on your mind unless you're entering your marriage bed with your wife. If you're not married, this switch is to be sealed under lock and key.

SEX SHOULDN'T BE ON YOUR MIND UNLESS YOU'RE ENTERING YOUR MARRIAGE BED WITH YOUR WIFE.

Every time you have a sexual thought, you allow your sex switch to be turned on and you wander into off-limits territory. Never allow this switch to be on when you're outside your covenant marriage bed. Otherwise, you're purposely inviting a disaster to come wreak havoc in your life.

How does this tie into *stay away*, *flee* and *escape*? I'm glad you asked! Outside of marriage, when your sex switch is turned off, you're in **stay away** mode. If your switch is turned *on*, you must immediately **flee** and turn it *off*. If you don't *flee*, look for His **escape**.

CHAPTER 23
IS SEX A PHYSICAL NEED?

Drink water from your own cistern and
running water from your own well.
Should your fountains be dispersed
abroad, streams of water in the
streets? Let them be only your own,
and not for strangers with you.
Let your fountain be blessed and
rejoice with the wife of your youth.
As a loving deer and a graceful doe, let
her breasts satisfy you at all times;
and always be enraptured with her love.

Proverbs 5:15-19

Let me be clear regarding the message of this chapter: Sex was created to exist inside a covenant marriage between one man and one woman. This chapter isn't talking about the "need" for sex inside a marriage. Go all out with your wife! Thirst for her and allow yourself to be enraptured by her. She is your one and only *cistern*–your sole source of sexual fulfillment in your life. Allow that to sink deeply into your soul. The "need" I'm referring to is the excuse men often give regarding their sexual immorality. Nowhere in the Bible and nowhere in science is sex cited as a physical necessity for human survival. Yet, "physical need" is the most common excuse men give for masturbation, pornography, fornication, affairs and all other sexual sin.

LUST ACTIVATES THE FLESH.

How do you convince a man sex isn't a physical need? What about a man who claims he is at the point of physical pain due to constant erections? What about unmarried men who don't have the option for sex? Or what about married men who, for whatever reason, are unable to engage in sex with their wives for a period of time? Most of these men might naturally conclude sex is a physical need and therefore justify their actions, right?

Here's the plain and clear answer: Lust activates the flesh. Think about that. In other words, quit believing the lie you can lust and not thirst, or look and not touch. If you allow lust to activate your flesh, you are sending a message to your flesh: *Prepare for sex.*

For he who sows to his flesh will of the flesh reap corruption, but he who sows to the Spirit will of the Spirit reap everlasting life.
Galatians 6:8

Lust is the fiery dart I referred to earlier. It leaves a residue in the mind and infiltrates the flesh. So, what's the solution? Simple. Follow the first directive: *Stay away.* Proverbs 6 states, *"we were not designed to withstand fire!"* Proverbs 7 tells us, *"departing from evil will be health to our flesh."*

Please catch this! Sex isn't something you physically need to survive. It's the world that has proposed and implanted this into the minds of men. I've never seen anything in the Bible or science that says: *Man must have oxygen, water, food, and sex to survive.* A man who believes sex is a physical need will justify his sexual immorality to the point of believing it's not sin. His flesh has turned against him and is attempting to convince him he will self-destruct without it. Quit excusing your behavior by being unable to resist. Instead, wake up to the fact your flesh was never designed to be fireproof! When you lust outside your marriage bed, you drop a burning match into your mind that aims to catch your flesh on fire. When 1 Corinthians 6:18 tells us *"sexual sin is against our flesh,"* you must believe that by allowing it in, you sabotage your ability to resist. This is why many men, out of complete ignorance, believe sex is a physical need. Here's the biblical truth: Allow sexual temptation in, expect sexual sin out.

I was recently sharing the message of this book with a Christian man whom I've personally known for many years. In the middle of our discussion he felt the need to enlighten me to something of which he believed I was unaware. He said I might need to reconsider writing a book asking men to completely give up pornography. He proceeded to educate me that many Christian men use pornography to avoid physically cheating on their wives. He literally said I could be responsible for many divorces by encouraging men to completely rid their lives of all sexual fulfillment outside their marriage. In other words, he and many of his Christian friends ignorantly believe sex is a physical need. How foolish some become to justify their sin! Furthermore, this group of *wet matches* is gravely deceived by thinking God's grace excuses their sexual immorality.

In the seventies, Berl Kutchinsky, a criminologist at the University of Copenhagen set out to prove when the Danish government lifted restrictions on pornography, the number of sex crimes would decrease. Dubbed "The Safety Valve Theory," this study suggested if men were offered unrestricted access to porn, sexual crimes in society would decrease. Their theory: Because men "need" sex, let's give it to them in the form of porn to keep them from acting out in society. In the end, the study was labeled "inconclusive." In his article, *Pornography: A Biblical Worldview Perspective*, Kerby Anderson reveals that when the data was further evaluated, the study masked what would have been an increase in the number of rapes committed!

One scripture could have saved Mr. Kutchinsky a whole lot of wasted time! Proverbs 27:20: "*Hell and Destruction are never full; So, the eyes of man are never satisfied.*" The more you engage in sexual immorality, the deeper your flesh will hunger for it. In the next chapter, you will see not only does pornography fail to satisfy men, but rather it inflames them.

Do you believe sex is a physical need? Are you of the mindset God created men as uncontrollable sexual beasts? Christians with this mindset usually end up in a lukewarm state for God.

GOD CREATED SEX TO BE A BLESSING, NOT A SUSTENANCE.

Read Revelation 3:14-22 regarding the lukewarm church. I picture a church building full of Christian men coming and going, muzzled from becoming the men God created them to be. This is a dangerous arena too many Christians are trapped in today. They are muzzled from fulfilling the position of the pastor or spiritual leader of their home, the appointed role of a husband and father.

God created sex to be a blessing, not a sustenance. If you're hungry and a feast is freely presented to you, why wouldn't you sit down and partake? In the same way, sex feeds our fleshly appetites. It's not rocket science! Don't set yourself up for failure. If you view sex as a physical need, it will be like a drug your flesh convinces you it cannot live without. Furthermore, you will begin to seek it more frequently and in stronger doses. Sin never satisfies. Many men not only need to change their thinking about sex, they need a serious mental and physical detox in order to stand with solid footing again. Author Ted Roberts hit the nail on the head: *"It's not just a moral problem, it's a brain problem."* Sexual sin is unlike any other sin, it's against your flesh.

Please take a moment and read 1 Corinthians 6:12-20 before proceeding to the next chapter.

PART 4
THE WARNING

CHAPTER 24

TIME SENSITIVE

Today, Christian men who dabble in pornography walk alongside the gates of Hell, never intending to stay too long. Instead, they go there to get a quick fill of sin. They profess to be followers of Jesus Christ during these visits. Over the years, they become more desensitized in this routine. Due to the nature of sin never satisfying, they venture to explore a bit further and stay a bit longer. Thinking back to my NSX friend, I don't believe he ever fathomed one day he'd be dealing with child pornography.

Child pornography is trapping men all over the world. If you're addicted to pornography and haven't allowed yourself to believe you too could fall, even to such an unimaginable sickness, let me remind you one last time: "Therefore let him who thinks he stands take heed lest he fall" (1 Corinthians 10:12). Society mocked the audacity of Ted Bundy when he said pornography caused him to rape and murder women and children. That was thirty years ago. In 2016, it was confirmed that one of the most common characteristics amongst rapists and serial killers was an addiction to pornography. When Osama Bin Laden's computer was seized, guess what? Investigators found an extreme amount of pornography on it. A former U.S. Chief Intelligence Officer reported that computer hard drives seized from ISIS also contained as much as 80% pornography. In 2016, society laughed when the state of Utah declared pornography a public health hazard. One article stated Utah's declaration was an "old-fashioned" morals bill driven by ignorance and bias. And don't forget chapter six: The Weinstein incident, the porn addict's Las Vegas massacre, and the celebration of Hugh Hefner, all occurring in a three-week period!

ONLY A FOOL BELIEVES HIS FLESH CAN RESIST A FIRE THAT HAS DEVOURED OTHERS BEFORE HIM.

If you currently view pornography but believe you're innocent compared to these examples, the enemy has you exactly where he wants you. If you believe you can continue in the same sin these guys started out with and not become just like them, you're a fool. Only a fool believes his flesh can resist a fire that has devoured others before him. Yes, your sexual sin is likely far less extreme than the examples in this book. However, please consider this a wake-up call. Sexual sin is always a downhill road to destruction.

I was sharing the s.a.f.e. directives with a close friend in the beginning stages of writing this book. As we talked about the struggles men face today, he said it distinctly reminded him of hearing David Wilkerson many years ago talk about how one day there was going to be a "box" that would take pornography to an "unimaginable level." Many

THE MAJORITY OF MEN TODAY ARE PORN ADDICTS.

thought this so-called box was the cable box, or the modem, which brought the Internet into our homes. These two boxes certainly took pornography to a more accessible level from mere magazines and videos. Now, full disclaimer. I'm not stating Wilkerson was some modern day prophet. I personally lean toward the biblical interpretation that God-breathed prophesy through man is something that likely ceased with the twelve Apostles. I do however believe Wilkerson was a true believer who had the Holy Spirit and was anointed to preach to and admonish believers to stay on the narrow path. I personally believe Wilkerson possessed God-given wisdom to discern the times. Daniel 2:21 says *"He changes the times and the seasons; He removes kings and raises up kings; He gives wisdom to the wise, and knowledge to those who have understanding."* As I sought the Lord further regarding the urgency or time-sensitive call to write this book, I began to wonder about this "box." Is there something on the horizon coming to take pornography to an unimaginable level?

The majority of men today are porn addicts. Yes, the majority. How can I make such a statement? In chapter nine, I referenced a study conducted by Pure Desire Ministries that showed 68% of Christian men viewed pornography on a regular basis. So, if most Christian men are regularly viewing porn, then it's safe to say that at least 68% of non-Christian men are doing the same. That's a majority. Sexual content is the most sought-after content on the Internet today. Men do not be deceived. This world is not in favor of your moral being; it is increasingly against it. It's Jesus himself who warns us: *"If you were of the world, the world would love its own. Yet because you are not of the world, but I chose you out of the world, therefore the world hates you"* (John 15:19).

If the world hates us, wouldn't it make sense for it to increase its attacks on us? Allow me to reiterate: I believe the enemy's number one attack on men today is sexual sin. Furthermore, this attack is rapidly increasing. The 21st century is known as the *Postmodern Era,* or the *Information Technology Age.* History and research have shown us technology advances exponentially. There's some debate and controversy on whether it's truly possible to sustain the speed of growth we've been experiencing. It's an understatement to say we've seen more advancement in technology in the last ten years than probably the last 1,000 years combined. Just think of your phone. It wasn't that long ago when the only "app" on your phone was a calculator! Through rapid advancement in technology, pornography has become more available and accessible to anyone who seeks it, and sadly, even to those who don't. Could the warning of a "box" be accurate? If so, have we already seen it? Was he referring to the cable box? Or was it the computer? Or is it the phones we all carry around? Have any of these boxes taken pornography to an "unimaginable" level?

THE WARNING OF A BOX

CHAPTER 25

> *"Teachings build us, but*
> *warnings save us."*
>
> ~ John Bevere

As I continued to seek the Lord regarding the time-sensitivity of this message, the warning about a certain box coming to take pornography to an "unimaginable level" kept resurfacing in my mind. As I studied the exponential advancement of technology, I quickly began to agree there was certainly something on the horizon and felt a sense of duty to warn others.

Pause: Pray before proceeding.

Before you proceed any further, please take a moment and ask God to help you digest the truth and stay vigilant to pursue purity as you finish these last few chapters. Ask God to help you absorb the warning set forth here without your flesh becoming too curious about all the details. Unlike many books written on sexual temptation, I purposed to write this book with the hope it would never tempt the reader. Most times, just reading or hearing the word "sex" activates the flesh of a man. This alone should illustrate how weak our flesh is! Unfortunately, the material ahead can cause your imagination to wander just by reading it. Turn off your sex switch!

God expects you to overcome. Again, *"No one engaged in warfare entangles himself with the affairs of this life, that he may please him who enlisted him as a soldier"* (2 Timothy 2:4). As you read the next few chapters, picture yourself as a kingdom soldier on a reconnaissance mission. The purpose? To prepare the way for yourself and others coming behind you. Proceed with caution and vigilance.

THE BOX

Way back in 2014, Facebook purchased Oculus for two billion dollars. Why? Read this excerpt from *Business Insider:*

Mark Zuckerberg believes that the Oculus headset could be the next widely adopted computing platform. His thinking is that first there were PCs, then there were PCs connected to the Internet, now there's mobile, and next there will be something else – a new communication platform." He thinks that something else could be virtual reality. "One day," said Zuckerberg, "we believe this kind of immersive, augmented reality will become a part of daily life for billions of people."

By the time you read this, most of you will have already heard about the rapid advancements being made in VR (virtual reality). In fact, some of you have already obtained a VR headset—most likely for gaming. Virtual reality is the time sensitive warning in this book. Specifically, *VR porn.* Believe it or not, it is already here, and

VR WILL TAKE PORNOGRAPHY TO AN UNIMAGINABLE LEVEL, ONE THAT MAY BE UNRECOVERABLE.

God is sending us an urgent warning. VR will take pornography to an unimaginable level, one that may be unrecoverable. I believe the box Wilkerson may have envisioned is VR. In April 2016, one of the top porn companies gave 10,000 free pairs of VR headsets to its frequent users and launched a VR category with 30 videos. By the end of 2016, the site saw 38 million searches for VR content.

The two purposes of this book are to lay out the S.A.F.E. biblical directives and to sound the alarm on VR. The directive of *stay away, flee,* and *escape* all sexual temptation is meant to shine light on God's parameters to avoid sexual sin. The time-sensitive warning is to sound the alarm on the hidden trap being laid before all of us. If you don't withdraw from pornography now, VR porn is set to permanently incapacitate you. Mark Zuckerberg believes it will be the next computing platform, and the porn industry has gone all in as well. When a man experiences VR porn, it will be like he blindly walked right into the hands of Satan himself. Incapacitated by it, he won't be able to resist crossing into the gates of Hell. As Proverbs 7:23 says, *"He did not know it would cost his life."*

I've previously said a Christian man who struggles with pornography is a man who walks alongside the gates of Hell just to look, knowing he will eventually walk away. Let me ask you a question. Why would a man who currently struggles with pornography not give VR porn a try? I mean, if you're already viewing pornography, what's the difference viewing it via VR? Is looking at porn on your phone less of a sin than VR? Let's say you're in the middle of viewing pornography and an offer to try VR porn presents itself. All you must do is either allow them to send you a free VR headset, order one, or strap on the one you may already own. I haven't found a single man who feels there is any degree of "sin difference." What's the point I'm trying to make? Viewing porn by VR versus on a screen will not carry any type of punishable sin difference–because there is no sin difference. Whether you're looking at it on the screen of your computer, your TV, your phone, or through VR, it's all sexual sin. However, just because there is no sin difference, do not be fooled. The difference is a hidden line. A line I believe God is warning if you cross it, you may never return.

The Hidden Line
Joseph Addison Alexander

There is a time, we know not when,
A point we know not where,
That marks the destiny of men
To glory or despair.

There is a line by us unseen,
That crosses every path;
The hidden boundary between
God's patience and his wrath.

To pass that limit is to die–
To die as if by stealth;

It does not quench the beaming eye
Or pale the glow of health.

The conscience may be still at ease,
The spirit lithe and gay;
That which pleases still may please,
And care be thrust away

But on that forehead God has set,
Indelibly a mark
Unseen by men, for men as yet
Are blind and in the dark

And yet doomed man's path below
May bloom as Eden bloomed;
He did not, does not, will not know,
Or feel that he is doomed

He knows, he feels that all is well,
And every fear is calmed;
He lives, he dies, he wakes in hell,
Not only doomed, but damned.

Oh, where is this mysterious bourn
By which our path is crossed;
Beyond which God himself hath sworn,
That he who goes is lost.

How far may we go on in sin?
How long will God forbear?
Where does hope end, and where begin
The confines of despair?

An answer from the skies is sent,
"Ye that from God depart,

While it is called today, repent,
And harden not your heart."

The Hidden Line was published by Joseph Addison Alexander in 1837. It has also been titled, *The Destiny of Man,* or *The Doomed Man.* If you blew right past the poem, I seriously hope you will go back and read it. It's a profound warning and I believe it can open your eyes to the devastation ahead. Now, I understand you may refute me if I were to say this poem, written almost 200 years ago, is a direct warning against VR porn. I get it. That would be a tough sell! However, I do know God is desperately trying to get the attention of His children. The moment I first read this, I couldn't help but believe it directly applied to the time-sensitive warning of VR porn. I sense Satan is expecting an all-out assault to capture all who come to the gates of Hell, especially for pornography. VR porn will be a newly installed hidden line at the gates of Hell.

Years ago, I heard Kirk Cameron and Ray Comfort on the radio telling a horrific true story about two guys on snowmobiles. It was so vivid, I don't think I'll ever forget it. Two guys were out snowmobiling in a wide-open meadow when one of them spotted an untouched, tree-lined, powdery path with two large wooden posts at the end of the path. Beyond the wooden posts, appeared to be another enticing wide-open

SATAN IS EXPECTING VR PORN TO BE A KNOCKOUT PUNCH, AND GOD IS WARNING US TO NOT EVEN BE IN THE ARENA.

meadow. So the young man immediately sped down the path to go check it out. When his snowmobile crossed through the two wooden posts, his life on this earth was over. Positioned at just the right height, a razor thin wire strung between the posts instantly decapitated him.

Today, you can freely view pornography, sin sexually, leave, and repent. It's a wide-open meadow most men visit frequently. Soon men will discover a new path with an enticing view ahead. When you enter by VR (the hidden line) you will be on a path that may cost your life. I'm not saying you cannot *escape*. I know and believe God will chase after all His children until the end. However, John 10:10 clearly tells us *"Satan is out to steal, kill, and destroy."*

Men, if you employ the biblical directives in this book, you can overcome all sexual sin in your life. However, you must act as fast as you can. I sense Satan is expecting VR porn to be a knockout punch, and God is warning us to not even be in the arena.

BEYOND HELL'S GATES

Jeremy Bailenson is the founder of the Virtual Interaction Lab at Stanford University and the co-founder of STRIVR, a leading commercial VR application company. Here's an excerpt from an interview he did with CBN news:

Virtual reality is not a media experience. When it's done well, it's an actual experience. In general, our findings show that VR causes more behavior change, causes more engagement, causes more influence than other types of traditional media. Virtual reality is potentially more addictive than video games and smartphones. Virtual reality is consuming. You put it on, you're there. It's really intense and you actually feel like you are there. In fact, it's so intense that VR goggles are not recommended for children under 13 and users are encouraged to take breaks every 30 minutes. It's a powerful tool. That power of the experience doesn't come for free. In the wrong hands, technology can be good; it can be bad. Uranium can heat homes and it can destroy nations. And virtual reality is a medium–it's up to us to use it for good. We have not yet evolved, the brain hasn't, to really understand the difference between a compelling virtual reality experience and an actual one.

As further evidence of VR's potential, read what Mark Zuckerberg said regarding his two-billion-dollar investment in VR:

The incredible thing about the technology is that you feel like you're actually present in another place with other people. People who try it say it's different from anything they've ever experienced in their lives. Oculus's mission is to enable you to experience the impossible. Their technology opens up the possibility of completely new kinds of experiences.

Regarding his first VR porn experience, Raymond Wong, senior tech correspondent for Mashable.com, said: "I'm an advocate for all new technologies that push video mediums to the next level, and after trying out VR porn, I don't think anyone who experiences it will be able to go back to 2D porn. It's that realistic." An executive of an adult video company said, "VR is the best way to satisfy people's sexual needs. It will give us a new option in our sexual life," he said.

Although the adult industry tends to be a bit opaque when it comes to actual statistics, data shows interest in VR porn far outpacing searches for virtual reality games, movies, or sports. Searches for "VR porn" jumped nearly 10,000% in less than two years, according to Google Trends data. During the 2016 Christmas season when VR first hit the mainstream technology market, Google reported searches for VR Porn jumped 50%. Analysts at research firm *SuperData* predict virtual reality could turn into a $40 billion business by 2020. They said the demand for virtual porn is evidence in favor of that outlook. If you're surprised by the suggestion porn is going to be what fuels VR, you must be unaware it is what currently fuels the Internet. Anna Lee, president of a leading adult entertainment company, confirmed this when she said: "Porn is the driving force right now that is actually causing the VR headset sales."

Men, if I could activate an *Amber Alert* and cause all the phones around the world to flash a warning against this, I would. Please be warned. If you're struggling with pornography today, you must kill it, before VR kills you. It's your last chance.

A WARNING TO ALL VIDEO GAME PLAYERS

In a 2018 article titled: "The World's Largest Porn Company is Targeting Your Children Through Video Games," Steve Warren of CBN news reported: "Porn is tightening its grip on America's youth through two major areas—online gaming and virtual reality." Men, this is an urgent warning. You, your children, or your grandchildren who play video games will be the first consistent VR users. In chapter six, I asked men to evaluate what kingdom fruit video games yielded in their lives. With VR on the horizon, why would you engage in a fruitless activity with the extreme potential to incapacitate you in sexual sin? Sensuality is already mainstream in video games today. With VR, it is only going to intensify.

Beyond video games, these headsets will be the initial way to engage in VR applications. Industry experts are pointing toward our phones becoming the primary portal for VR technology down the road. This means everyone will eventually be face-to-face with this technology. You might be thinking I'm a bit over-the-top. Trust me, I tried to finesse this in such a way that I didn't lose or turn anyone off from reading it. I agree, even as Christians, it is viewed as legalistic or extreme to choose not to engage in the "normal" activities of our day. However, today's extreme times will require extreme sacrifices. If you're going to live a Godly life, you're going to have to start making decisions to

TODAY'S EXTREME TIMES WILL REQUIRE EXTREME SACRIFICES.

"set yourself apart from this world" (Romans 12:2, 1 Peter 2:9).

Alistair Charlton of *The International Business Times UK* said this: "I don't want to suggest VR porn will genuinely cause the end of civilization and make us all live our lives plugged into the Matrix, but after the initial shock and giddiness subsided, it was difficult not to wonder if we've somehow taken a step too far."

GOING IN FOR THE KILL

CHAPTER 27

*With her enticing speech
she caused him to yield,
with her flattering lips
she seduced him.
Immediately he went after her, as
an ox goes to the slaughter,
Or as a fool to the correction
of the stocks.
Till an arrow struck his liver.
As a bird hastens to the snare,
he did not know it would cost his life.*

Proverbs 7:21-23

In our house, it's a rare occasion to sit down and watch a movie. The *stay away* directive usually cancels out most of the garbage on TV today. However, my wife and I recently came across and watched *Temple Grandin*. It's a true story about an autistic woman who revolutionized the livestock processing industry. Okay, I know that sounds insanely weird, but trust me, it's a great movie.

Ms. Grandin is largely credited with the design and methodology most slaughterhouses still use to load and guide livestock through the slaughtering process. Her success hinged on studying the movement patterns of cattle based on their anxiety levels. She spent countless hours identifying which activities spooked them and which calmed them. Before, when a cow was being led to the slaughter, it sensed the danger it was headed toward. This caused the cow to react and it would attempt to escape or avoid the path it was on. Because of this, the process was time-consuming and often chaotic. Under Grandin's design, all the factors alerting the cow it was heading toward danger, were eliminated.

IF YOU THINK FREEDOM FROM PORN IS TOUGH TODAY, WAIT UNTIL YOU GET BLINDSIDED BY VR PORN.

Calmly, willingly and unknowingly, cows began stepping toward their death.

If you're a Christian, you know pornography is wrong and you don't want to engage in it. I believe many of you fight against it and truly desire to escape it. Sometimes you have victories, other times you don't. It's a chaotic process and Satan has been spending a lot of time watching men deal with it. He's been studying sexual sin since the beginning of time. He knows the tendencies of our flesh. VR will be Satan's going-in-for-the-kill move. If you think freedom from porn is tough today, wait until you get blindsided by VR porn. Men who enter porn by VR are going to do so calmly, willingly and unknowingly. Men, the alarm is blaring! *Stay away, flee,* and *escape* now. A time is rapidly approaching when you may be too far down the chute, and it could cost your life.

The "time sensitive" alarm this book is sounding is VR porn. However, it is only the beginning of Satan's attack. The continual advances in VR, such as augmented reality (AR), will become the real killers. You see, if VR walks a person through Hell's gates, AR will be the fiery dart that keeps them there. What's the difference? Without spending the next several pages doing a technical comparison, allow me to put it as simple as I can. VR takes you outside of your present environment into an entirely new virtual one. AR brings virtual reality and applies it to your present environment. Thus, making the experience more convincing. Some synonyms of the word augment are *intensify, reinforce, swell, escalate, supplement,* and *inflame.* AR porn will *inflame* a person. Some of the technology being developed on the AR side include bodysuits, robots and hologram boxes. What is the goal? Remember what VR expert Jeremy Bailenson said, "We have not yet evolved. The brain doesn't recognize the difference between a compelling virtual reality experience and an actual one."

The entire goal of VR is to make an experience so real your brain convinces you it is. Today, most pornography companies are fully engaged in developing VR/AR content. Why do I write about it with such fervency? Why is this a time sensitive warning? Because I sense God is shining a spotlight down for us to avoid the edge of a cliff many are about to walk off of.

To deliver you from the immoral woman, From the seductress who flatters with her words, Who forsakes the companion of her youth, And forgets the covenant of her God. For her house leads down to death, And her paths to the dead; None who go to her return, Nor do they regain the paths of life.

Proverbs 2:16-18

"VR is a question for us because it's not just interactive, but immersive, so it has the potential to be even more seductive for people who are prone to addiction," says Michael Rich, a Harvard University pediatrician and founder of the Center on Media and Child Health in Boston. The damaging effects of VR porn are set to become crippling. Worse, you're not likely to return from it. VR porn is a path to death.

Death? What does that mean? For starters, death in your relationship with Christ, death to your marriage and death to your role as a father to your children. Once the enemy destroys your relationships, he will destroy you. I write with fervency because we are dealing with fire–Hell's fire. A Christian man who struggles with sexual immorality today is like a man with a dormant infection. His body has yet to alert him his life is in danger. When this man takes his struggle into VR, the dormancy period will abruptly end. The disease will activate and overtake him. His chances of survival will be fleeting at best.

PART 5
UNMUZZLED MEN

CHAPTER 28

FIRE MACIE

> *Deliver those who are drawn toward death and hold back those stumbling to the slaughter.*
>
> Proverbs 24:11

"Hey, I want you to meet Macie," Clay hollered as I entered the office building one Monday morning. Clay occupied the first suite in the building where I worked. "She's my new assistant," he said. Without being completely rude, I quickly said hello and jetted off to my office. With one swift glance at Macie, I saw she was an attractive young woman. As I sat at my desk, an entire scene went through my head involving Clay. It had probably been about a year since he and his family moved to Texas. I had just helped him with a vehicle purchase. He was so appreciative of our service, I would frequently hear him in the hallway singing our praises to clients who came in and out of the building. His Christmas card that year featured him, his wife, and their two young boys all dressed in their new Texas-themed attire. He was quickly living up to a bumper sticker which reads: *I wasn't born in Texas, but I got here as quick as I could!* As I sat there, I couldn't shake it. The scene going through my head was of Clay being unable to resist a moment of temptation with Macie.

I finally shook it off as a ridiculous assumption and decided to surrender it to the Lord in prayer. The day began and, as usual, it flew by. Walking down the hallway toward the exit, I heard Clay, "See you J" followed by another soft "Bye" from his new assistant.

The next morning, I quickly walked past Clay's office, purposely trying to avoid a situation that seemed so obviously wrong. Week after week, my frustration grew. It was obvious to me, yet I seemed to be the only one who saw it. How could a man take fire like that every day? Macie was an attractive young woman who sat in the same small office with Clay every single day. Worse, I began to see them return from lunch together—in his car.

One morning, I began to feel as a true Christ-follower, I'm suppose to alert this man. I quickly dismissed the thought and convinced myself I was assuming the worst of this guy. After all, I was assuming Clay would fall to temptation, have an affair, and one day inform me he and his wife were getting a divorce. This scene was burned in

"I WANT YOU TO CALL IT OUT."

my mind since the day he first introduced me to Macie. A few days later, I found myself asking God in prayer what He wanted me to do with this burden. I couldn't let go that I was suppose to act. As I tried to discern God's direction in prayer, my mind kept telling me: *"There is no one else in this building willing to do it. God is asking you to do it."* Well, if this was God leading me, I knew He was right about that. I couldn't think of anyone who regularly passed through that hallway, who would ever make such a radical assumption, and boldly (or stupidly) carry out something like this. As the days passed, I began to wonder–*what if it was God asking me to intervene?*

I decided to go away for a night to the cabin I frequented on my annual sabbaticals. One Friday afternoon, I packed an overnight bag and headed off. Sure, I was hoping to use this time as a mini sabbatical, but my primary purpose was to pray and seek the Lord on behalf of Clay. Upon arriving, I entered the cabin and got situated. I sat down with my Bible and entered God's presence through prayer and worship. I surrendered myself to the Lord and immediately pressed Him to unravel my crazy assumptions regarding Clay. *Lord, please forgive me for assuming the worst of this guy. Will you show me your truth regarding this situation and reveal why I feel so burdened by it? Amen.* As soon as I opened my eyes, I felt immediately I was to tell Clay to fire Macie! I then of course questioned if this was Holy Spirit leading me or my own frustration. "I'm going to tell a man to fire his assistant because he isn't strong enough to resist her and will one day fall to her? He is going to think I assume the worst of him," I said out loud as if I were talking to God in the cabin. I sunk in my chair and thought: *If this isn't God, I'm in trouble. If it is God, Clay is in trouble.*

As you grow deeper with the Lord, you begin to sense His Spirit in greater measure. You begin to make real decisions based on prayer, His ways and His Word. Many times these decisions don't make worldly sense, and they are usually difficult and sacrificial to make.

"Okay, I'll do it." I said to God in prayer. After months of witnessing the situation and not being able to shake the Holy Spirit calling me to action, I felt confident it was the Lord and it was not me simply assuming the worst of a guy. As I pressed into the Lord, I made a protocol. Step 1: Text Clay and invite him to lunch. Step 2: Tell him to fire Macie. Step 3: Do it now. So, that night I texted Clay and asked him to lunch. I felt a sense of urgency to get this done. Now remember, this was a Friday night and Clay and I were really nothing more than office mates. "Sure. How about Monday?" he quickly texted back. He didn't even ask why. He just enthusiastically accepted. It was all set and I was confident God was at work. It felt as if I received a direct order from God, and like a military soldier, I was committed to carrying it out—regardless of the outcome.

A man who is intimate with God is not intimidated by man.

~ Leonard Ravenhill

The following Monday, Clay texted: "You ready?"

Before exiting my office, I went to the Lord in prayer and surrendered myself. I prayed for the Holy Spirit to lead us both. As Clay and I walked outside, he asked what I was driving. That day, it was a Porsche 911 (a perk of owning your own car business). Without hesitation, he decided he would ride with me.

At lunch, a full hour passed by and I still hadn't delivered the directive. I learned a lot about Clay. He was a believer, a successful businessman, and in the prime of his life. As my flesh began to convince me I was a fool to think so lowly of this guy, I received a text on my phone. I glanced over at it and let out a quick "Ha." Clay inquired, "What is it?"

"Oh nothing, just a question I often get asked. *Are you hiring anyone?*" I said.

"You should hire an assistant," he spouted.

As he said this, Isaiah 30:21 flashed through my mind: *This is the way, walk in it.* It was as if God Himself caused that text, at the exact moment, with the exact question to open a door for me to carry out my directive.

"That's right," I said. "You recently hired Macie. How's it working out?"

"So far so good. As soon as she gets up to speed on the nature of our business, it will be even better." he said.

"Clay, can I ask you a man-to-man question? Do you find Macie attractive?" I immediately and confidently jabbed (with sweat dripping down both my armpits)!

"What? Ah...I mean...wait, do you?" he fumbled back.

"Yes. She is very attractive," I admitted.

"Yeah, I know. She definitely could dress a bit more professionally," he laughed.

His comment confirmed my directive and so I *bit*.

I told him about the scene that played through my mind the first day I met Macie. I explained I was so burdened by it all I went away just to pray about what to do. Then with a short pause, a quick breath, and sweat still dripping down my armpits, I delivered the directive: "Clay, fire Macie"

As I prepared for him to punch back with: *What? Who do you think you are?* I took a deep breath and immediately felt a huge flood of peace. "Wow. That's heavy," he slowly muttered back. It was as if the burden literally left me and transferred onto him! I don't remember much about what I spoke after that. However, I couldn't help but think how God's love and His Word just flowed through me with such authority.

As we entered the parking lot, I think it hit us both at the same time: *Oh yeah, we rode together.* Yep, awkward! We didn't talk much until we were just about to pull into the office parking lot.

"What if you were to meet Macie, go to lunch and get to know her? Do you think it would change your perspective?" Clay suggested. "I'm definitely not going to do that!" I quickly responded. "Furthermore, this isn't about me or what I think. I only did it because I believe God was leading me." I said.

Just as he was about to get out of the car, he told me about a business trip he had coming up in Las Vegas. He went on to say that once he got back, he would put some thought into all of this.

"Las Vegas? Is she going with you?" I asked.

"Whoa, it's not like that. It's a business trip." he quickly countered.

The sense of urgency I had at the cabin immediately came to my mind: *Step 3: Do it now.* I texted Clay from the cabin not because I was afraid I would forget or never do it; I did it because I felt a sense of urgency to do so. I began to press Clay a little further.

"Is your wife going with you?" I asked.

"No, but dude please, nothing is going to happen. I'm not like that," he uncomfortably laughed.

"Are you flying there together or staying at the same hotel?" I pressed.

"Dude? Calm down. Why are you acting like this?" he asked.

I then told him something I hadn't yet shared. "It was your boys. In the scene that played through my head, I saw them growing up without their dad." I said. I don't think he knew what to say, so he genuinely thanked me for my concern, and we both went back to work.

Looking back, I can't shake it was a setup from the enemy when Clay hired Macie. What a victory it would have been for Satan. Not only would it destroy a marriage, it would've taken a father away from two young boys who desperately love and need their dad. The following week, I received a text from Clay:

Macie showed up late twice this week. I had to fire her.

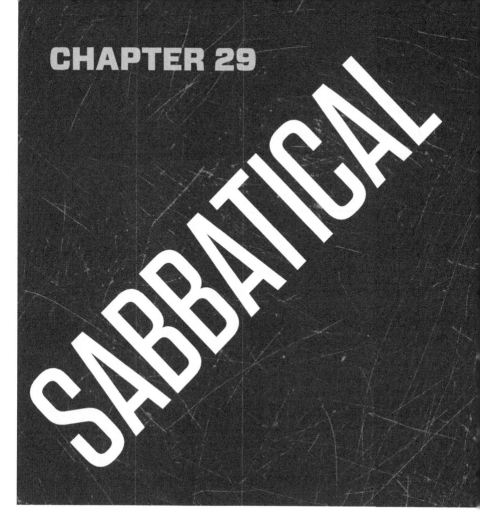

CHAPTER 29

SABBATICAL

The first time I heard the word *sabbatical* was in college. A professor informed the class he would be filling in for the regular professor who was away on *sabbatical*. Many years later, the term resurfaced when my home group leader encouraged me to take a sabbatical to spend time with God and His Word. At the time, I couldn't fathom doing it. Me? Schedule time off, book a place to stay, leave my wife—all to somehow meet with God? My flesh didn't want to do it, my mind didn't want to acknowledge it, but my spirit knew I desperately needed it.

My first sabbatical will forever be etched in my mind. To save money, I pitched a tent at a Texas state park. Besides what sounded like lions, tigers, and bears outside my tent all night, (oh, and the random mountain man who showed up in the park bathhouse at midnight while I was doing my business), it was just me and God for two days!

The next year, I opted to rent a small fishing cabin at a nearby lake. It was on this sabbatical my life changed. In prayer, I sensed the Holy Spirit: *"You were made for a purpose, and I'll get you to your destination. Will you surrender everything to me?"* So I did. I truly decided to go all in with God. I surrendered my life, my marriage, my vocational calling, and my future. As I pondered this change in my mind, I pictured myself in a hot air balloon. I remember gazing at this picture in my mind, ready to set sail in the winds of the Lord. My balloon gently swayed in the air, with only one tether holding me down. Staring at that tether, all my excitement drained out of me as if all the air was being let out of that balloon.

You see, I had surrendered everything I could physically and mentally surrender (pride, anger, greed and all my past sins). The one tether staked in the ground was one I had attempted many times to be released from for years, but never could. I battled the tether of sexual immorality year after year. I pleaded with God to be released from it countless times. *Lord, please remove my fleshly desires. Give me eyes for my wife only. Help me! Change me!* Year after year, I attacked that tether and did everything I could think of to be released from it. I read books, listened to sermons, had accountability and even went through a private deliverance session at my church. When I saw this picture in my mind, I was devastated to think I could spend the rest of my life "grounded" while knowing God had an entire itinerary planned out for me. It was sobering to imagine everything I was created to be and do was out there waiting for me, but a single restraint could hold me back from it all. Men, can I tell you this is exactly the goal of Satan. He wants to stop you from reaching God's destiny for your life.

Driving to the office one day, I heard a pastor on the radio who was sharing about his struggle to quit smoking. Between services at his church he would go hide and sneak in a quick smoke. One day his father-in-law caught him. He looked at him, put his hand around his shoulder, and delivered a *tether-severing* word. "Don't let a tiny little thing like that keep you from the big things God has for you." The pastor went on to share how it was the last time he held a cigarette in his hands.

Sexual immorality cuts off the wings that lift us toward the highest, richest, most durable joy.

- John Piper

Just one tether can hold the entire purpose of a man hostage. Sadly, there are men living in the latter days of their life still tethered to the ground. What happens to a man who dies tethered to the ground by a habitual sin? I'm not only talking about salvation here; rather, I'm wondering about the look on the Father's face when that man dies. Like a gift never unwrapped and enjoyed, the fullness of all God planned and hoped for him is never realized. What does God say to a son who was harnessed by sin his whole life?

The Creator of the world designed us to inhabit this earth for only a vapor of time. He has gifted us to fulfill specific initiatives for the glory of His kingdom. It is time to wake up and start attacking this life with a holy boldness! God's plan for your life is at stake and he doesn't intend for you to die tethered to the ground. In his book, *Killing Kryptonite*, John Bevere nails it

JUST ONE TETHER CAN HOLD THE ENTIRE PURPOSE OF A MAN HOSTAGE.

when he says, "Don't treat strongholds in your life casually when God's empowered you to demolish them."

If you have never done a sabbatical, schedule it and commit to completing it! If Jesus went away to be with His Father, how much more should we? On our website, <u>UnmuzzledMen.com</u>, there is a guideline regarding sabbaticals. I wouldn't be where I am today if I hadn't began going away to spend time alone in prayer and in His Word.

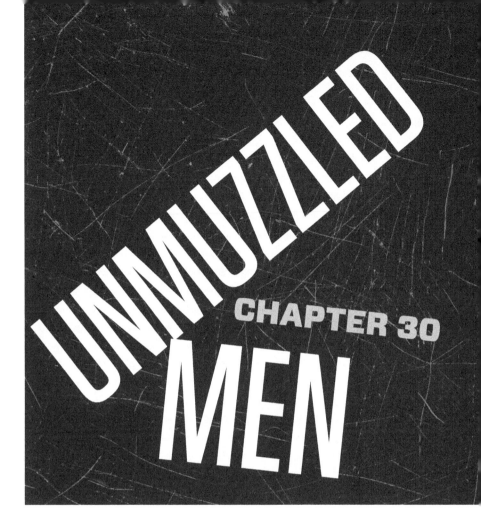

UNMUZZLED MEN

CHAPTER 30

How much more would a few good and fervent men affect the ministry than a multitude of lukewarm ones?

~Oecolampadius

In the movie *A Knight's Tale* starring the late Heath Ledger, there is a scene where Ledger's character hesitantly agrees to test out some new body armor his blacksmith made for him. As soon as he sees it, he immediately rejects that it will protect him. The normal armor worn by knights was much thicker and weighed at least twice as much as this new armor. The young blacksmith challenges his rejection and asks if he at least has the courage to test it. The next scene shows Ledger's crewmates speeding toward him with a massive wooden beam. As soon as the beam strikes him, he is thrown into the air and falls flat on the ground. His crew frantically looks down to check on him.

"I didn't feel a thing!" he shouts. The following scene shows Ledger confidently strutting over to mount his horse. As he walks past the other knights, they immediately take notice of his armor and begin to laugh. In the background, there are knights attempting to mount their horses, but they need the full help of their crew due to the bulkiness of their armor. When they all see how Ledger quickly and gracefully mounted his horse, all their laughter immediately ceased. It was as if he wasn't wearing any armor at all.

I believe the armor of God is a lot like this. Simply put, God has given us everything we need to succeed. Ephesians 6:10-20 tells us to put on this spiritual armor. I think many Christian men read and agree with it, but in the end, don't believe enough to put it on.

Imagine a package showing up at your doorstep. As you open it, you find a set of armor and a note that reads: Son, I made this specifically for you. Put it on and keep it on. It contains my power. It will protect, bless and lead you while you're on the earth. Love, God. Do you realize everyone who genuinely accepts Jesus Christ as their Lord and Savior receives this? Ephesians 6:10-18 states:

Finally, be strong in the Lord and in his mighty power. Put on the full armor of God, so that you can take your stand against the devil's schemes. For our struggle is not against flesh and blood, but against the rulers, against the authorities, against the powers of this dark world and against the spiritual forces of evil in the heavenly realms. Therefore put on the full armor of God, so that when the day of evil comes, you may be able to stand your ground, and after you have done everything, to stand. Stand firm then, with the belt of truth buckled around your waist, with the breastplate of righteousness in place, and with your feet fitted with the readiness that comes from the gospel of peace. In addition to all this, take up the shield of faith, with which you can extinguish all the flaming arrows of the evil one. Take the helmet of salvation and the sword of the Spirit, which is the word of God. And pray in the Spirit on all occasions with all kinds of prayers and requests. With this in mind, be alert and always keep on praying for all the Lord's people. (NIV)

Men, the plans He has for us require His supernatural armor! This isn't some Easter or Christmas outfit either! Christianity isn't some accessory item you wear around. I can't tell you how many times I've seen a man wearing a cross as his eyes lustfully watch a woman passing by. Or what about a man who goes to church Sunday morning and is sexually immoral Sunday night? What if the reason you're not experiencing the freedom God has for you is because you're not wearing your armor full-time?

Maybe you're deceived and wearing some knockoff armor. Think of all the different "armors" men use to deal with sexual temptation: Software protection, accountability, medication, willpower, or cheap grace. Without full submission and obedience to God and His Word, these will fail your flesh! God's armor is the only solution designed to protect you against the fiery darts of Satan.

We have entered a critical juncture in regard to sexual sin. If the preachers warning of the box or *The Hidden Line* poem have anything to do with sexual sin, we're about to enter a nuclear war zone. His armor will be the only way to survive. Here's an illustration to consider. If 15% of the world population is completely sold out for God and 15% is completely sold out against God, the remaining 70% is either unsure about God or lukewarm for God. Listen up. A time is nearing in which the 70% will be forced to decide which side they're on. Meaning, soon you will either be all in with God or all in against God. In other words, no more middle ground.

WE'RE ABOUT TO ENTER A NUCLEAR WAR ZONE. HIS ARMOR WILL BE THE ONLY WAY TO SURVIVE.

Picture a drawbridge crowded with men. The bridge begins to open and slowly separate. The men on the bridge start to scramble trying to decide which side to run toward. Some make last minute jumps from one side to the other. Other men seem to be trying to pull away from one side but appear to be anchored down by it. This is a picture of the new trap set before us: VR porn. If you don't make the decision to leave behind all sexual immorality in your life, VR porn will anchor you down. A man who falls victim to the unimaginable level of pornography via VR is going to wake up one day in the blistering fires of his sin, unable to fathom ever being released from it. In 2 Peter 3:10, the Bible warns us this world is decaying; don't go crumble with it. Detach from all sexual immorality and do it now. Today, porn muzzles a man. Tomorrow, VR porn will put him in a straitjacket. Which one do you think is easier to escape?

Those who have the privilege to know have the duty to act.
- Albert Einstein

Every week, I have clients in and out of my office. Once as one client was leaving, I leaned into the hallway to invite the next clients in. This couple instructed their two middle-school-aged children to stay in the waiting area outside my office. As I introduced myself and began to close the door, I was immediately burdened for the children. The burden arose from a stack of magazines one of the other tenants in the building had put in the shared waiting area. Most of them were the standard women's fashion and celebrity gossip magazines. In my opinion, today, these aren't far off from pornography. I didn't want those children to innocently flip through those magazines and see things God never intended their eyes to see. So, I put them where they belonged: The trash. A few days later, I approached the tenant who supplied the magazines and admitted I threw them away. She forgave me and admitted she never thought about such issues.

As I share story after story with the Christian men in my circles, I'm burdened by the lack of response to the onslaught of sexual immorality constantly before us. Men, as Christians, we're the only ones on this earth who will ever take a stand against this garbage. You know the announcement a flight attendant makes before a plane takes off?

Ladies and gentlemen, in case of an emergency, an oxygen mask will drop down in front of you. Please secure your mask first before assisting others.

I can't shake that God is making a similar announcement:

Men, there is a slaughter ahead of you. Unmuzzle yourself first and then go grab a hold of others.

This isn't simply a proposal of this book, it's a biblical commandment:

Brethren, if a man is overtaken in any trespass, you who are spiritual restore such a one in a spirit of gentleness, considering yourself lest you also be tempted. Bear one another's burdens, and so fulfill the law of Christ.
Galatians 6:1-2

God is calling a generation of men to rise up and get unmuzzled! Once your connection to God is restored and you're walking in freedom, I believe the Holy Spirit will lead you to those He is calling you to grab hold of.

Brethren, if anyone among you wanders from the truth, and someone turns him back, let him know that he who turns a sinner from the error of his way will save a soul from death and cover a multitude of sins.
James 5:19-20

A few years ago, I was privileged to attend a meeting for an organization that feeds, shelters, and clothes children all over the world. During the message, the organization's founder, recited Isaiah 40:31: *"But those who wait on the Lord shall renew their strength; They shall mount up with wings like eagles, they shall run and not be weary, they shall walk and not faint."* He went on to talk about eagles for a bit. He said eagles don't avoid turbulence, they seek it out. Eagles know turbulent winds only cause them to go higher and fly faster. This immediately resonated with me. As I have strived to be all I can be for God, I've realized I desire to go higher with God and be faster to act for God, especially when the turbulence is rough. I feel as if I'm a soldier for the Kingdom of God, and I want to fulfill my duty and not miss the mark. I'm often reminded of that time I felt the Holy Spirit leading me to act on behalf of my friend Clay: *"There is no one else in the building who is going to do it. God is asking you to do it."*

How shall I feel at the judgment, if multitudes of missed opportunities pass before me in review, and all my excuses prove to be disguises of my cowardice and pride?
- Dr. W.E. Sangster

What if God has positioned you to intercept someone before Satan claims a victory? What if He who has *"equipped you for every good work"* is waiting for you to be free so He can use you (2 Timothy 3:17)? Do you realize He intends to involve you in reaching His people? Most men I encounter say they believe this but struggle to take action. I love the NLT version of 2 Timothy 2:21: *"If you keep yourself pure, you will be a special utensil for honorable use. Your life will be clean, and you will be ready for the Master to use you for every good work."* 1 Thessalonians 5:14 says, *"Now we exhort you, brethren, warn those who are unruly, comfort the fainthearted, uphold the weak, be patient with all."* Men, God has created us to need one another for both encouragement and reproof. James 5:16 says, *"Confess your trespasses to one another, and pray for one another, that you may be healed. The effective, fervent prayer of a righteous man avails much."*

GOD'S PATIENCE IN MY COWARDICE

For several years, I had the privilege of being a part of a special prayer service at my church and on occasion I was invited to speak from the pulpit. On one of those nights, the pastor turned toward me to see if I wanted the say anything. I quickly signaled to him that I didn't. Like most nights, I would press into the Lord for this service and more times than not, I would sense the Holy Spirit leading me to share. This night was no different. However, when I told the pastor no, I was denying something I felt I was suppose to share. Confused and frustrated, I immediately began praying. I asked God to give me another chance if I had missed the mark. I asked Him to forgive me if it was my own cowardice declining to deliver His message.

After the service, as I was walking down one of the aisles, I was drawn to a certain young man sitting in the back of the sanctuary. I approached him, introduced myself and told him the Holy Spirit may have highlighted him to me. He was caught off guard as you might expect and responded with: "Okay, thank you. What for?" I really didn't have a response, so I said: "I don't know. However, is there anything you need prayer for?" I've come to accept sometimes God will just point you toward someone.

MANY CHRISTIANS MISS OPPORTUNITIES BECAUSE THEY DON'T STEP OUT IN FAITH.

Many Christians miss opportunities because they don't step out in faith and love for one another. They feel led to talk to someone but quickly squash it if it feels uncomfortable or they have something specific to say. I've learned to trust the Holy Spirit is real and will lead me. I never want to miss an opportunity to be a useful utensil for God.

As you might expect, this young man was caught off guard. I then asked if anything was blocking his connection to God. "No, not that I can think of," he said. I sensed, by his demeanor and body language, he was holding back. So, I pushed a little, "So there is nothing blocking your connection to God?" I'll never forget his timid response. "There may be one thing, I guess. I've been struggling with same-sex attraction." Wow. I'll never forget this moment with this young man. Why? This was the exact topic I cowardly declined to speak on from the platform just minutes before! Standing on the platform, I was terrified, especially in the world we live in today, to go in front of a crowd of over a thousand people and say, "*Hey, I believe God wants to minister to someone here tonight struggling with same-sex attraction.*"

True obedience is the refusal to compromise in any regard our relationship with God, regardless of the consequences.
~ **A.W. Tozer**

Two things happened that night. First, I was able to share God's amazing love with this young man. I shared how the Holy Spirit put this on my heart to share from the platform just twenty minutes before. I admitted I didn't have the courage to deliver it from the platform. Then I said to him, "But God cared enough about a certain young man He sent me right to him." His countenance immediately changed. He couldn't help but smile! Second, my faith was radically increased!

A raging fire still ignites inside me as I think back to the missed opportunity to intercept another man Satan was quickly closing in on. From the day I turned on the music in that NSX to the day my friend was arrested, more than a year had passed. If only I had been spiritually alert and ready. I've replayed the scene in my head countless times since. Today, my response would have been different: *Wait, this kind of music doesn't sync with who I think this guy is. From what he has shared, he loves the Lord, his wife and children. The garbage in this music isn't feeding that love, it's poisoning it. Something isn't right. God, use me.*

Instead, I did nothing.

Is it possible God could have used me to intercept this man? Or was it simply a coincidence one of God's children who was harnessed and being led to the slaughter, came to see me about a car? Was it also a coincidence the car was an NSX, my dream car? To date, it's still the only NSX I've ever dealt with. Was it a coincidence that CD was playing when I started the car? What about the fact that I started a car business purely based on prayer and seeking the Lord's Will? Was all this just one big coincidence?

What could I have done anyway? Met him for coffee, pull out that CD, *bite* and expose Satan's grip on his life?

You better believe it.

What about you?

CONCLUSION

MARCHING ORDERS

> *If you have no desire to bring others to heaven, you are not going there yourself.*
>
> ~ Charles Spurgeon

Today, I encounter muzzled men all the time. Instead of overlooking their muzzles, I often approach them to see if they're aware of it. In the flesh, it creates about the same awkwardness as telling someone they have a piece of lettuce stuck in their teeth. In the Spirit, it's like performing open-heart surgery on them.

And have no fellowship with the unfruitful works of darkness, but rather expose them.

Ephesians 5:11

As men, we're to become kingdom-minded soldiers directed by God to first overcome sin, and second, to intercept and redirect other men from sin. I began this book by saying men aren't leading the charge in this area because they can't give what they don't have. Look at Proverbs 24: *"hold back those stumbling to the slaughter."* Imagine a bear attempting to rescue a cub heading toward a cliff. The only way it could physically do it would be to bite onto the cub and pull it back. If you're muzzled, you can't *bite!* Are you catching this? Remember my NSX friend? What if God was calling me to be the man who could've bitten and pulled him away from the cliff? As I look back today, I'm devastated I didn't recognize the opportunity to act. Even more discouraging, apparently no one else did either. In an area widely known as the *Bible Belt* and in the megachurch where this guy was a member, was there no one else ready, willing, or unmuzzled to be an agent for God on this man's behalf? There is no doubt in my mind God had been trying to save him. God is trying to reach all His children, no matter what their circumstances.

About a year ago, I met a firefighter at a truck auction. Many firefighters have side businesses they run on their days off. This guy was no different, and he was looking for a truck for his business. Upon meeting and chatting with him for a bit, I spotted his muzzle. His sheepish passivity gave it away when I asked if he was a believer. So, I *bit* and called it out. Without hesitation, he told me he struggled with pornography. I explained the muzzle and how it was blocking his connection to God. I told him how it prevented him from being the husband and father he was called to be. I walked him through the directives of staying away, fleeing, and God's supernatural escape. Lastly, I warned him about the "hidden line" of VR porn. He looked at me like a deer in headlights! Of course, I did just fully expose a secret he'd been hiding for twenty years, preached at him for twenty minutes, all while holding him hostage in the beating hot sun! With few words, he thanked me for sharing and quickly departed. About a month later, our paths crossed again.

"Hey, remember me? I wanted to let you know I destroyed that muzzle. I repented to God and confessed everything to my wife. It was insanely difficult and humiliating to do, but it freed me from the grip Satan had on me. I'm a S.A.F.E. man now. Thank you for calling me out."
- An unmuzzled firefighter

Men, God is poised with His empowering grace to sever the straps of all those who are muzzled. He calls us to be more than conquerors while on this earth. Christianity is not some life insurance policy that comes with an "I'm a Christian" name tag. What's that going to do? According to Ephesians 6, true men of God wear armor, not name tags. Do you have sexual sin in your past or present? Are you ready to believe God is willing to move Heaven and earth to lead you out of it? Do you believe Satan is completely against you and the destiny God has planned for you?

Men of all ages, the time to lay down your muzzle is now. We're living in perilous times, and God will use as many kingdom soldiers as He can get. Today, there is a shortage of unmuzzled Christian men. Not

HAVE YOU EVER THOUGHT GOD'S HANDS WERE TIED FROM BLESSING YOU?

only will eradicating sexual sin supernaturally bless you, I believe God will supernaturally position you to *bite* and grab hold of others around you.

Is hidden or unconfessed sin holding you back? If so, I'm *biting* right now. I'm calling it out as you read this sentence. I'm not condemning you; I'm exposing the enemy's grip on you. If you have unconfessed sexual sin (past or present), or any related sexual struggle, Satan has a grip on you. Have you ever thought God's hands were tied from blessing you? Do you feel unworthy to approach Him? This muzzling grip is hell-bent on preventing you from obtaining all God has for you and the destiny He created you to fulfill.

Rise up men of God and start believing enough to get yourself off this destructive road! God has made a way of *escape* from the grip of sexual sin. If you say you believe, act now. 2 Chronicles 7:14 says, "*If My people who are called by My name will humble themselves, and pray and seek My face, and turn from their wicked ways, then I will hear from heaven, and will forgive their sin and heal their land.*" No matter what your sin is, God is ready to revive and replenish all that has been lost or stolen from you. Every man of God can overcome and conquer sexual sin. Start believing and walking as the *unmuzzled man* that God created you to be.

To all fathers and future fathers: You are responsible for relaying the truths and warnings in this book to your children. Not the church, not the school, not the government, and most definitely not this world! Unmuzzle yourself so you can warn your children of Satan's grip.

A FINAL WORD

The simple statement, 'God is for us', is in truth one of the richest and weightiest utterances the Bible contains.

~ J.I. Packer

Confess your sins, repent, and accept God's grace. It's there to redeem and empower you to live righteously on this earth. True repentance is God's only path to redemption. If you're married, you must confess <u>all</u> hidden sin to your spouse. This is not optional or case specific. God's light must infiltrate your marriage covenant for the darkness to be eliminated. It is important you begin to pray for your spouse to receive your confession. Don't just go blurt it out to her. Spend some time with the Lord and pray for His grace to cover your situation. Seek wise counsel to help guide you and pray for you. Your wife is going to need His supernatural grace and presence to properly receive this confession. If you're not married, *"confess to someone in your life"* (James 5:16). This confession is not merely a biblical formality; it's a spoken, supernatural sword that severs the enemy's grip on you.

Once you've confessed your sins, accepted His grace, and are cleansed by the blood of Jesus, immediately put the s.a.f.e. directives into practice. Daily, ask God to go before you and prepare a path of purity before you. Practice, practice, practice the act of *staying away*. This must become a vigilant act of obedience in your life. Don't ever forget: *Fleeing* is always more difficult than *staying away*.

I also encourage you to ask God to reveal times in your past when He supernaturally intervened to offer you an *escape*. In those times, did it cross your mind God could be trying to save you? Study missed *escapes*, so you can better discern His presence going forward. His *escape* isn't some "get out of jail free" pass! Instead, it's meant to reveal the supernatural manifestation of God in your life. This will fuel you to become vigilantly against sexual sin!

CONFESSION IS NOT MERELY A BIBLICAL FORMALITY; IT'S A SPOKEN, SUPERNATURAL SWORD THAT SEVERS THE ENEMY'S GRIP ON YOU.

FINAL WORDS

Be vigilant and hate sin as God hates sin.
This will transform you from a flesh-pleasing man
to a God-pleasing man.

UNMUZZLEDMEN.COM

Please consider posting a review online! Your review could cause another man to turn away from the slaughter he's headed toward.

I encourage you to ask God to start using you to grab hold of others around you who are heading toward the slaughter. Maybe it's as simple as giving them this book. Join in this calling and allow God to use you to help sever the straps of muzzled men all over this world.

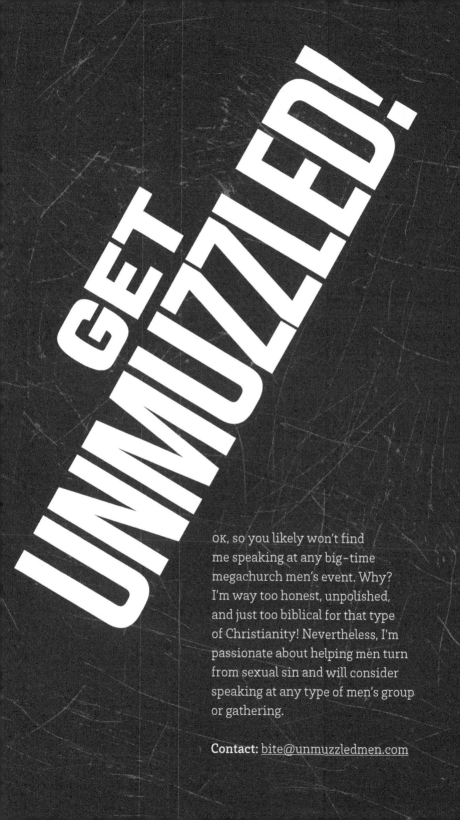

GET UNMUZZLED!

OK, so you likely won't find me speaking at any big-time megachurch men's event. Why? I'm way too honest, unpolished, and just too biblical for that type of Christianity! Nevertheless, I'm passionate about helping men turn from sexual sin and will consider speaking at any type of men's group or gathering.

Contact: bite@unmuzzledmen.com

APPENDIX

S.A.F.E.

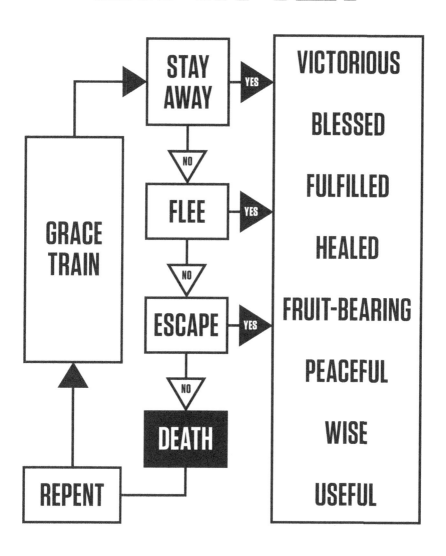

HOW TO RECEIVE, RECOGNIZE & RESPOND TO GOD'S ESCAPE

1. **Be in right standing with the Lord.**
» *For My eyes are on all their ways; they are not hidden from My face, nor is their iniquity hidden from My eyes.* (Jeremiah 16:17)
» *The Lord is far from the wicked, but He hears the prayer of the righteous.* (Proverbs 15:29)
» *He who pleases God shall escape from her, but the sinner shall be trapped by her.* (Ecclesiastes 7:26)
» *The righteous is delivered from trouble.* (Proverbs 11:8)
» *For You O Lord will bless the righteous; with favor You will surround him as with a shield.* (Psalm 5:12)
» *Righteousness guards him whose way is blameless, but wickedness overthrows the sinner.* (Proverbs 13:6)
» *He is a shield to those who walk uprightly; He guards the path of justice and preserves the way of His saints.* (Proverbs 2:7-8)
» *No one engaged in warfare entangles himself with the affairs of this life, that he may please him who enlisted him as a soldier.* (2 Timothy 2:4)

2. **Humble yourself in His sight.**
» *Humble yourselves in the sight of the Lord, and He will lift you up.* (James 4:10) It takes a truly humble man to be at the point of giving in to sexual sin, only to turn away and surrender himself in the sight of the Lord. I love what Leonard

Ravenhill once said: *"He who kneels before God will stand in any situation."*

» *What then shall we say to these things? If God is for us, who can be against us?* (Romans 8:31)

» *Therefore let him who thinks he stands take heed lest he fall.* (1 Corinthians 10:12)

» *For if we sin willfully after we have received the knowledge of the truth, there no longer remains a sacrifice for sins.* (Hebrews 10:26)

» *God resists the proud, but gives grace to the humble.* (James 4:6)

3. **Be alert and look for His escape.**

» *The way of a lazy man is like a hedge of thorns, but the way of the upright is a highway.* (Proverbs 15:9) If you're not physically or mentally alert, you will get trapped. However, if you pause, get up and walk away before falling into sin; you may spot his *escape.*

» *Watch and pray, lest you enter into temptation. The spirit indeed is willing, but the flesh is weak.* (Matthew 26:41) Be alert. You must be aware and sometimes even ask for an *escape.*

4. **Physically move.**

» *Your ears shall hear a word behind you, saying, "This is the way, walk in it."* (Isaiah 30:21)

» *But be doers of the word, and not hearers only, deceiving yourselves. For if anyone is a hearer of the word and not a doer, he is like a man observing his natural face in a mirror; for he observes himself, goes away, and immediately forgets what kind of man he was. But he who looks into the perfect law of liberty and continues in it, and is not a forgetful hearer but a doer of the work, this one will be blessed in what he does.* (James 1:22-25)

NOTES

CHAPTER 2

Sproul, R.C. American Reformed theologian, Ligonier Ministries, www.ligonier.org

McDowell, Josh. "Alarming Epidemic: Porn the Greatest Threat to the Cause of Christ" CBN News interview with Mark Martin, April 2016

Barna Research Group / Josh McDowell Ministries. "The Porn Phenomenon: A Comprehensive New Survey on Americans, The Church, and Pornography" December 2016

Lifeway Research, Nashville, TN. Research Release, "Americans Worry About Moral Decline, Can't Agree on Right and Wrong."

https://news.gallup.com/poll/235280/americans-say-pornography-morally-acceptable.aspx

https://www.afa.net/the-stand/culture/2018/07/new-push-for-pedophilia-just-another-sexual-orientation July 2018

CHAPTER 3

Sowell, Thomas. American economist

Patrick F. Fagan, Ph.D., Senior Fellow and Director of the Center for Marriage and Religion Research, Family Research Council, Washington, D.C. "The Effects of Pornography on Individuals, Marriage, Family, and Community." December 2009

Leonard Ravenhill. "Why Revival Tarries" Bethany House, 1959, 1987 ISBN 0764229052

CHAPTER 4

Begg, Alistair. Truth For Life Ministries, https://www.truthforlife.org/

Bonhoeffer, Dietrich. "The Cost of Discipleship." Touchstone; 1st edition, September,1995 ISBN 0684815001

Pennington, Tom. Author & Pastor, https://countrysidebible.org/

Spurgeon, Charles Haddon. (1834-1892) Baptist Reformer Wikipedia

CHAPTER 5

Lloyd-Jones, Martyn. Welsh Minister, https://www.mljtrust.org/

Evans, Jimmy. Author & Pastor, https://xomarriage.com/

CHAPTER 6

https://www.foxnews.com/us/arizona-high-school-football-player-faces-70-charges-for-photo-prank May 2016

Dobson, James. Focus on the Family, "Fatal Addiction: Ted Bundy's Final Interview." January 1989

Weinstein, Harvey. Academy Award-Winning Film Producer. Wikipedia. November 2017

Hefner, Hugh Marston. Founder, Playboy Magazine. Wikipedia

https://abcnews.go.com/US/las-vegas-gunmans-computer-child-pornography-disturbing-search/story?id=52467413

http://www.latimes.com/local/la-me-weinstein-surrender-case-20180525-story.html May 2018

CHAPTER 7
Washer, Paul. American Protestant Christian evangelist, https://heartcrymissionary.com/

https://www.foxnews.com/health/compulsive-video-game-playing-now-qualifies-as-mental-health-condition June 2018

Alter, Adam "Irresistible: The Rise of Addictive Technology." Penguin Press, March 2017 ISBN 1594206643

Bilton, Nick. "Disruptions: Steve Jobs Was a Low-Tech Parent" The New York Times. September 2014

Ravenhill, Leonard. "Why Revival Tarries" Bethany House, 1959, 1987 ISBN 0764229052

CHAPTER 8
Tozer, Aiden Wilson. Author and Christian Evangelist. "The Pursuit of God." Aneko Press; Updated Edition July 2015 ISBN 1622452968

CHAPTER 9
Pure Desire Ministries. Ongoing study collected by Pure Desire Ministries Intl. 2009 to present. Participants of study completing SAST - R V2.0 © 2008, P. J. Carnes, Sexual Addiction Screening Test - Revised.

Barna Research Group / Josh McDowell Ministries. "The Porn Phenomenon: A Comprehensive New Survey on Americans, The Church, and Pornography" December 2016

Andrews, Andy. "The Noticer" Thomas Nelson, April 2011 ISBN 078523232X

Chiara Sabina, Janis Wolak, and David Finkelhor. CyberPsychology & Behavior. "The Nature and Dynamics of Internet Pornography Exposure for Youth." December 2008

Focus on the Family Poll, October 2003

McDowell, Josh "The Perfect Storm: Confronting the Greatest Youth Crisis of the 21st Century" Josh McDowell Ministries October 2013

CHAPTER 10
Piper, John article: https://www.desiringgod.org/interviews/how-have-you-processed-the-sin-of-ravi-zacharias

CHAPTER 11
https://en.oxforddictionaries.com/definition/fireproof

CHAPTER 12
Packer, J.I. English-born Canadian evangelical theologian

Emanuel James "Jim" Rohn (1930 –2009), American entrepreneur, speaker and author. Wikipedia

Dr. Norman Doidge M.D. "The Brain That Changes Itself: Stories of Personal Triumph from the Frontiers of Brain Science" Penguin Books, December 2007 ISBN 0143113100

Sullum, Jacob. "The FBI Distributes Child Pornography to Catch People Who Look at It." Reason.com, August 2016

John Bunyan (1628 –1688), preacher and author. Widely known for the Christian allegory: Pilgrim's Progress. Wikipedia

Hall, Dudley. https://lifetoday.org/connect/words-of-life/what-should-we-do-when-we-fail/

CHAPTER 13
Begg, Alistair. Truth For Life Ministries, https://www.truthforlife.org/

CHAPTER 14
John, Owen, Kelly M. Kapic, Ph.D., Justin Taylor, Ph.D. Overcoming Sin and Temptation. Crossway, Redesign Edition, March 2015 ISBN: 1433550083

CHAPTER 15
Edwards, Jonathan. 18th Century American revivalist preacher, philosopher, and Congregationalist theologian

https://www.foxsports.com/boxing/story/floyd-mayweather-manny-pacquiao-fight-to-take-place-may-2-in-las-vegas-022015 February 2015

CHAPTER 18
Dietrich Bonhoeffer (1906 –1945), German theologian and author. Wikipedia

Ferguson, Sinclair. Scottish theologian

Booth, William (1829 –1912), 19th Century Evangelist and Founder of The Salvation Army. Wikipedia

CHAPTER 20
Roberts, Ted. Former U.S. Marine Corps Fighter Pilot, Host of The Conquer Series and Author of Pure Desire. Bethany House Publishers; Revised, Updated ed. edition, April ,2008 ISBN: 0764215663

McGee, J. Vernon. American minister, Thru the Bible Ministries, https://www.ttb.org/

Bonhoeffer, Dietrich. "The Cost of Discipleship." Touchstone; 1st edition, September,1995 ISBN 0684815001

https://www.divorcelawyersformen.com/blog/divorce-rate-us-2018/

CHAPTER 23

Kutchinsky, Berl. "The Effect of Easy Availability of Pornography on the Incidence of Sex Crimes: The Danish

Experience," Journal of Social Issues 29 (1973): 163-81.

Kerby Anderson, "Pornography – A Biblical Worldview Perspective", www.probe.org/pornography May,2016

CHAPTER 24

Hall, Allan; Newton, Jennifer "Laptops recovered from ISIS jihadists are filled 'up to 80%' with PORN, reveals former US intelligence director" Mailonline.com and DailyMail.com, July 2016

McCombs, Brandy. "Utah leaders call pornography a plague damaging young minds" Associated Press, April 2016

Wilkerson, David Ray. (1931-2011) Author, Christian Evangelist and Founder of Teen Challenge and Times Square Church.

CHAPTER 25

Bevere, John. "Good or God: Why Good Without God Isn't Enough" Messenger International, August 2015 ISBN: 1933185945

Carlson, Nicholas. "Facebook Bought Oculus Because It Thinks Virtual Reality Will Follow Mobile as The Next Great Computing Platform." BusinessInsider.com, March 2014

Zuckerberg, Mark. Founder, Facebook.com

https://techcrunch.com/2017/01/06/a-whole-lot-of-people-watched-vr-porn-in-2016 January 2017

Alexander, Joseph Addison. 19th Century Biblical Scholar. "The Hidden Line." Aka "The Doomed Man," Aka "The Destiny of Man" First published in the Sunday School Journal, Philadelphia, PA, April 1837.

CHAPTER 26

Bailenson, Jeremy. Professor and Founding Director of Virtual Human Interaction Lab at Stanford University and also Co-founder of STRIVR Labs, Inc.

CBS News. "How virtual reality can change how you act toward others." Cbsnews.com, May 2016

Zuckerberg, Mark. Founder, Facebook.com, https://fr-fr.facebook.com/zuck/posts/10101319050523971 March 2014

Wong, Raymond. "VR porn is here and it's scary how realistic it is." Mashable.com, January 2016

Nash, Charlie. "Virtual Reality Porn Developer: 'VR is the Best Way to Satisfy' Sexual Needs" Breitbart Tech, Breitbart.com, November 2016

Nickelsburg, Monica. "Virtual reality porn is just foreplay: Why augmented reality is the future of adult entertainment" GeekWire.com, November 2016

Grubb, Jeff "Google Searches for "VR Porn" Increased Nearly 10,000% in 17 Months" VentureBeat, July 2016

SuperData. https://www.superdataresearch.com/virtual-reality-forecast March 2016

Lee, Anna, President, Utherverse.

https://www1.cbn.com/cbnnews/2018/october/how-the-worlds-largest-porn-company-is-targeting-your-children-through-video-games October 2018

Charlton, Alistair "Virtual reality porn: Tried, tested and intensely creepy" International Business Times, March 2015

CHAPTER 27
Gerson, S. E., Jackson, M., Ferguson, S., Monger, C., Johnson, W. M., Danes, C., O'Hara, C., Warner Home Video (Firm). (2010). *Temple Grandin*. New York: HBO Home Entertainment.

Bailenson, Jeremy. https://charlierose.com/videos/28609 August 2016

Michael Rich, MD, MPH, Associate Professor of Pediatrics at Harvard Medical School, Associate Professor of Social and Behavioral Sciences at the Harvard School of Public Health.

CHAPTER 28
Both names in this chapter have been changed to protect the privacy of the individuals.

CHAPTER 29
Piper, John. DesiringGod.org, "Husbands, Lift Up Your Eyes: Letter To A Would-Be Adulterer" July 2017

Bevere, John. "Killing Kryptonite: Destroy What Steals Your Strength" ISBN 1937558118 October 2017

CHAPTER 30
Oecolampadius, Johannes. 15th Century Protestant Theologian and Reformer. Wikipedia

Helgeland, B., Van, R. T., Black, T., Ledger, H., Addy, M., Sewell, R., Bettany, P., Columbia TriStar Home Entertainment (Firm), (2001). *A Knight's Tale*.

Ledger, Heathcliff Andrew (1979 –2008) Academy and Golden Globe winning Australian actor and director.

Einstein, Albert. 19th Century Nobel Prize Physicist. Wikipedia

Sangster, William Edwin. 19th Century Methodist Reformer.

Tozer, Aiden Wilson. Author and Christian Evangelist. "The Pursuit of God." Aneko Press; Updated Edition July 2015 ISBN 1622452968

MARCHING ORDERS
Spurgeon, Charles Haddon. (1834-1892) Baptist Reformer

A FINAL WORD

Oecolampadius, Johannes. 15th Century Protestant Theologian and Reformer. Wikipedia

PERSONAL NOTES

PERSONAL NOTES

PERSONAL NOTES

PERSONAL NOTES

PERSONAL NOTES

PERSONAL NOTES

PERSONAL NOTES

Made in the USA
Las Vegas, NV
04 April 2024